T0299224

Global Financialization and Corporate Innovation Strategy

Technological innovation is a core aspect of corporate and national competitiveness and it is not only complex—requiring cooperation and coordination among many stakeholders—but it also involves high risk due to uncertainty. Financial markets are a key to successful technological innovation. This book looks at how traditional financing and non-traditional ones transform corporate innovation strategy.

This book reviews Korean companies to illustrate the impact of financialization on technological innovation through the relationships among financialization, managerial myopia, and short-termism of innovation strategy. It does so by conducting an empirical study using Korean firm and USPTO data from the period 2000 to 2019. By analyzing the innovation capabilities of Korean companies and presenting indicators of technological competitiveness, it offers insights into how financialization has influenced organizational behavior, causing them to shift strategy formulation, decision-making for production, investment, and technological innovation away from a long-term perspective to short-term one.

This concise book will be of interest to those interested in strategy and entrepreneurship innovation, especially policy makers focusing on financialization or national level innovation strategies.

Hwan Joo Seo is Professor at the Division of Business Administration at Hanyang University, South Korea. His research interests focus on Regulation theory, technological innovation, and financialization.

Sung Jin Kang is Professor at the Department of Economics and Director of the Institute for Economic Research, Korea University. His main fields of research are issues on sustainable development such as green growth, climate change, and economic development.

Routledge Focus on Business and Management

The fields of business and management have grown exponentially as areas of research and education. This growth presents challenges for readers trying to keep up with the latest important insights. *Routledge Focus on Business and Management* presents small books on big topics and how they intersect with the world of business research.

Individually, each title in the series provides coverage of a key academic topic, whilst collectively, the series forms a comprehensive collection across the business disciplines.

South African Business in China
Navigating Institutions
Kelly Meng

Privatisation in India
Journey and Challenges
Sudhir Naib

Global Financialization and Corporate Innovation Strategy
The Case of Korean Firms
Hwan Joo Seo and Sung Jin Kang

The Multiple Case Study Design
Methodology and Application for Management Education
Daphne Halkias, Michael Neubert, Paul W. Thurman and Nicholas Harkiolakis

For more information about this series, please visit: www.routledge.com/ Routledge-Focus-on-Business-and-Management/book-series/FBM

Global Financialization and Corporate Innovation Strategy

The Case of Korean Firms

Hwan Joo Seo and Sung Jin Kang

Routledge
Taylor & Francis Group
LONDON AND NEW YORK

First published 2022
by Routledge
4 Park Square, Milton Park, Abingdon, Oxon OX14 4RN

and by Routledge
605 Third Avenue, New York, NY 10158

Routledge is an imprint of the Taylor & Francis Group, an informa business

British Library Cataloguing-in-Publication Data
A catalogue record for this book is available from the British Library

Library of Congress Cataloging-in-Publication Data
Names: Seo, Hwanjoo, author. | Kang, Sung Jin, 1964– author.
Title: Global financialization and corporate innovation strategy: the case
of Korean firms / Hwan Joo Seo and Sung Jin Kang.
Identifiers: LCCN 2021056020 (print) | LCCN 2021056021 (ebook) |
ISBN 9781032147376 (hardback) | ISBN 9781032147383 (paperback) |
ISBN 9781003240822 (ebook)
Subjects: LCSH: Technological innovations–Korea. |
Financialization–Korea. | Business planning–Korea.
Classification: LCC HD45 .S4128 2022 (print) | LCC HD45 (ebook) |
DDC 658.4/063–dc23/eng/20211203
LC record available at https://lccn.loc.gov/2021056020
LC ebook record available at https://lccn.loc.gov/2021056021

ISBN: 9781032147376 (hbk)
ISBN: 9781032147383 (pbk)
ISBN: 9781003240822 (ebk)

DOI: 10.4324/9781003240822

Typeset in Times New Roman
by Newgen Publishing UK

Contents

vi *Contents*

Figures

Tables

Acknowledgements

It has been a great blessing and a pleasure for us to work with Routledge. We would like to thank the editors Mr. Kendrick Loo and Ms. Yongling Lam for their patience and guidance in navigating through the complexities of the times and the project and bringing it to completion. We are deeply grateful to Dr. Steven Bammel for his English proofreading and invaluable comments. An expression of gratitude is also extended to Sun Lee and Seon Ju Lee of the department of Economics, Korea University, for data acquisition and cleaning support. Their valuable suggestions and comments have made a lot of progress in our draft. Needless to say, we bear all the responsibility for all errors and viewpoints made in this book. As always, immeasurable thanks to our families: Min Hee, Tae Young, Jung Min, Hea Jun, Hee Chang, and Hyo Chang.

Abbreviations

AI	artificial intelligence
DB	data base
EPB	Economic Planning Board
EPO	European Patent Office
EVA	economic value added
FIRE	finance, insurance, and real estate
GDP	gross domestic product
IIP	international investment position
IMD	International Institute for Management Development
IoT	internet of things
IPO	initial public offering
IT	information technology
JPO	Japan Patent Office
KISVALUE	Korea Information Service Value
KOSDAQ	KOrea Securities Dealers Automated Quotation
KOSPI	KOrea Composite Stock Price Index
KSIC	Korea Standard of Industry Classification
M&A	mergers & acquisitions
NBER	National Bureau of Economic Research
NFCs	non-financial companies
NTIS	National Science & Technology Information Service
OECD	Organization for Economic Co-operation and Development
PCT	Patent Cooperation Treaty
R&D	research and development
ROE	return on equity
ROK	Republic of Korea
SMEs	small and medium-sized enterprises
S&P	Standard and Poor's
S&T	science and technology

USD	United States dollar
USPTO	United States Patent and Trademark Office
WCY	World Competitiveness Yearbook
WIPO	World Intellectual Property Organization

1 Introduction

Technological innovation is a major driver of corporate competitiveness and sustainable economic growth. Anderson and Tushman (1990) studied the US minicomputer, cement, and airline industries over several cycles of technological change, finding that technology evolves in four stages, or eras, and that these stages form a repeating cycle: (1) era of ferment, (2) era of dominant design selection, (3) era of incremental change, and (4) era of technological discontinuity. Breakthroughs—technological discontinuities—kick off a new start to the cycle, promoting uncertainty and environmental turbulence.

The advent of new technologies related to the so-called "4th Industrial Revolution," such as IoT (Internet of Things), AI (Artificial Intelligence), robot technology, and unmanned transportation, now signal a new era of ferment, a time when new technological breakthroughs are developed. Technological discontinuity, when new scientific and technological discoveries are made, opens windows of opportunity, allowing late-comers to catch up with established leaders. During the transition, the relative positions of leaders and laggards often change. Additionally, R&D spending is particularly risky during this period because new technological breakthroughs require large long-term financial investments, even though the returns on those investments are uncertain. Because the technological and economic potential of new technologies and the needs of consumers are not clearly known early in the cycle, information asymmetry about investments may lead to adverse selection and moral hazard.

Therefore, efficient financial markets are a prerequisite to ensuring that technological innovation can be sustained under uncertainty and continue into the next stages of the cycle. Financial markets ease financial constraints, reduce financial costs, ensure proper monitoring of managers, and allocate capital to projects with the greatest potential to result in new processes and profitable new technology commercialization

DOI: 10.4324/9781003240822-1

(Kerr and Nanda, 2015; Hsu et al., 2014; Pellegrini and Savona, 2017). As a result, academic interest is focused on the linkage between financial markets and the process of technological development.

However, two recent lines of research have demonstrated that excessive financial development can negatively impact technological innovation. The first mechanism of the negative effects of financial development on innovation is related to the "managerial myopia" hypothesis. Excessive pressure from the capital markets to raise short-term returns leads to managerial myopia, which holds back corporate investment in R&D—a high-risk, large-scale investment over a long period of time. This throttling of corporate investment ultimately suppresses corporate technological innovation (Narayanan, 1985; Stein, 1988 and 1989; Porter, 1992; Graham et al., 2005; Edmans et al., 2017). Graham et al. (2005) provide survey results showing that 78% of financial executives would sacrifice long-term value to meet short-term earnings targets. Edmans et al. (2017) assert that a CEO's concern about current stock price is associated with lower spending growth in R&D and capital expenditure. Stein (1988, 1989) and Porter (1992) conclude that managerial myopia results from takeover pressures imposed by institutional investors, who are impatient traders or speculators sensitive to fluctuations in stock prices and earnings. Hostile-takeover pressure—as well as the accompanying threats of being bought out at an undervalued price and of being ousted from leadership—compel managers to sacrifice long-term company interest for current profits (Kaplan and Minton, 2012).

In a climate of ever-present pressure by institutional investors, managers focus more heavily on short-term earnings targets set by capital markets, and this has led to widespread managerial myopia. Thus, when institutional investors push for higher short-term returns, managers forgo investments that would otherwise increase the long-term value of the firm. In summary, the argument from managerial myopia contends that the short-term interests of institutional investors have inhibited investment in innovation.

The second mechanism discussed in the literature through which corporate innovation may be held back is based on the "financialization" hypothesis. Financialization refers to the increasing importance of financial markets, financial motives, financial institutions, and financial elites in the operation of the economy and its governing institutions, both at the national and international levels, these trends having emerged primarily since the 1980s. As with managerial myopia, higher levels of financialization are also expected to act as a burden on technological innovation and economic growth.

Boyer (2000) and Stockhammer (2008) identify the growth observed in developed economies since the 1980s—along with the process of financialization—with a finance-led growth model, or a finance-dominated accumulation regime. However, the authors point out that this growth model is characterized by low investment by companies in tangible and intangible assets. Studies of financialization show that the shareholder-value orientation caused by financialization has led to managerial myopia, which, in turn, has resulted in sluggish investment in tangible and intangible assets (Lazonick and O'Sullivan, 2000; Aglietta and Rebérioux, 2005). In other words, the emphasis on maximizing shareholder value has moved corporate strategy and decision-making about production, investment, and technological innovation away from a long-term perspective and moved it toward short-termism.

Recent studies synthesizing the above managerial myopia and financialization hypotheses (Seo et al., 2012, 2020; Dosi et al., 2016; Jibril et al., 2018) have built on research into the relationship between financialization, managerial myopia, and technological innovation. This research looks at how deeper financialization negatively impacts investment in intangible assets, including R&D investment. These studies find that financialization can interfere with corporate innovation strategy through the following three channels (Figure 1.1).

First, pressure from capital markets on non-financial firms greater than ever (see ④ in Figure 1.1). Related to the rise of shareholder primacy and encroaching threat of hostile takeovers (see ①+②), this channel is discussed by Stein (1988, 1989), Porter (1992), Lazonick and O'Sullivan (2000), Aglietta and Rebérioux (2005), Orhangazi (2008), and Stout (2012). Hence, as capital market pressures rise, managerial myopia (see ⑤)—a perspective under which managers focus on short-term cash flow at the expense of value-creating long-term investment—becomes the norm. Under pressure to boost stock prices and short-term earnings, managers choose corporate strategies that increase dividends and stock-buybacks and eschew re-investments that would otherwise secure long-term competitiveness (see ⑥-1). Higher dividends and stock repurchases reduce the amount of net profit available for investment (see ⑦-1). Thus, firm investment in tangible and intangible assets, including R&D, drops (see ⑧-1). Stockhammer (2004), Orhangazi (2008), Demir (2009), and Davis (2018) find that managerial myopia has led to lower investment in tangible assets in both developed and developing countries.

Second, financial innovation has led to the development of quick-gain-oriented financial products (see ③ and ⑤). Thus, firms can now earn a greater proportion of their profits from financial assets. This

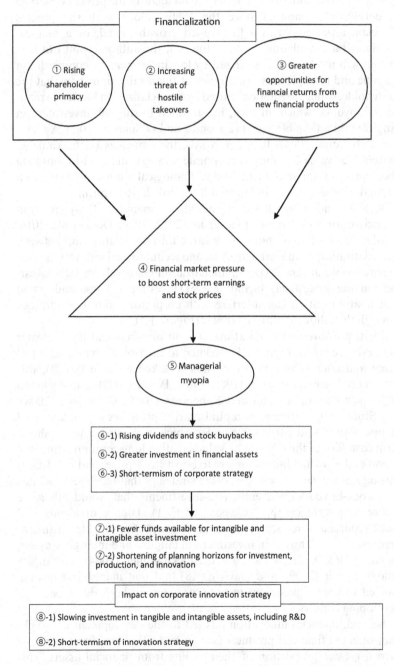

Figure 1.1 Managerial myopia and short-termism of innovation strategy.

encourages managers to favor financial instruments that deliver returns through interest, dividend income, and capital gains, and discourages managers from focusing on producing and selling products (see ⑥-2). As a result, investment in financial assets crowds out investment in tangible and intangible assets (see ⑦-1 and ⑧-1). Seo et al. (2012) and Jibril et al. (2018) use data on Korean firms (1994–2009) and Brazilian firms (94 manufacturers, 2011–2016), respectively, to show that financial investment has crowded out intangible asset investment.

Lastly, the rise of a shareholder-value orientation has oriented corporate innovation strategy toward a short-term perspective, putting less emphasis on the long term (see ⑦-2). Capital market pressure and shareholder impatience force managers to keep their eyes on short-term performance. As a result, managers adjust corporate strategy to policies that pursue incremental innovation delivering adequate results with lower R&D spending. In contrast to incremental innovation, radical (or fundamental) innovation does not contribute to business performance over the short-term, is highly risky, and demands large R&D investments over a long period of time before realizing value (see ⑧-2). Using OECD macroeconomic data (31 countries; 1990–2006) to study the relationship between financialization and innovation short-termism, Lee et al. (2020) find that, as managerial myopia intensifies in line with deepening financialization, economic entities direct technological innovation strategy toward incremental innovation at the expense of risky, long-term radical innovation.

The first two channels explain how financialization negatively impacts technological innovation by reducing investment in R&D and intangible assets. However, the third mechanism suggests that financialization can also change the nature of corporate innovation strategy itself. In other words, as the emphasis on shareholder value has promoted short-termism, firm strategy would be expected to have shifted toward incremental innovation (safe innovation focusing on gradual improvements) and away from radical innovation (risky innovation over the long term).

This book consists of five chapters, providing an overview of previous research on financialization and analyzing the innovation capabilities of Korean companies using various data and indicators. In addition, Chapter 2 includes a literature review on financialization, looking at related papers from a variety of social science fields—economics, business administration, politics, sociology—since the 2000s. The topic has typically been discussed in terms of the narrow relationship between financial market efficiency and technological innovation. However, Chapter 2 seeks to explore more comprehensively the interlinkages that connect the financial markets, corporate governance, and technological innovation.

Chapter 2 attempts to present a new perspective based on the relationships between the financial markets, corporate governance, and technological innovation. We attempt through this literature review to clarify the relationships between financialization and technological innovation, an approach that prior discussions on financialization overlook.

Chapter 3 analyzes the innovation capabilities of Korean companies by utilizing various data measures related to innovation input and output. Our input measures include R&D investment, R&D investment composition, and R&D personnel, while our output measures describe the number of patent registrations and patent citations. We conduct a qualitative analysis using patent data that simultaneously leverages the number of patent registrations, as well as the number of citations and degree of radicalness, doing so to support our conclusions.

In Chapter 4, we consider how financialization has influenced the technological innovation of Korean companies, doing so from the following three perspectives. First, we analyze how managerial myopia caused by financialization has impacted R&D investment by companies. Second, we analyze the impact of managerial myopia on corporate innovation strategy. Lastly, by comparing trends in Korea with trends in OECD countries, we attempt to verify whether the short-termism of innovation strategy is a phenomenon of Korean companies alone or whether such short-termism applies across OECD countries.

References

Aglietta, M. and A. Rebérioux (2005), *Corporate governance adrift: A critique of shareholder value*, Cheltenham: Edward Elgar.

Anderson, P. and M. L. Tushman (1990), "Technological discontinuities and dominant design," *Administrative Science Quarterly*, Vol. 35, No. 4, pp. 604–603.

Boyer, R. (2000), "Is a finance-led growth regime a viable alternative to Fordism? A preliminary analysis," *Economy and Society*, Vol. 29, No. 1, pp. 111–145.

Davis, L. E. (2018), "Financialization and the non-financial corporation: An investigation of firm-level investment behavior in the United States," *Metroeconomica*, Vol. 69, No. 1, pp. 270–307.

Demir, F. (2009), "Financial liberalization, private investment and portfolio choice: Financialization of real sectors in emerging markets," *Journal of Development Economics*, Vol. 88, No. 2, pp. 314–324.

Dosi, G., V. Revest, and A. Sapio (2016), "Financial regimes, financialization patterns and industrial performances: Preliminary remarks," *Revue d'économie industrielle*, Vol. 154, No. 2, pp. 63–96.

Edmans, A., V. W. Fang, and K. A. Lewellen (2017), "Equity vesting and investment," *The Review of Financial Studies*, Vol. 30, No. 7, pp. 2229–2271.

Graham, J. R., C. R. Harvey, and S. Rajgopal (2005), "The economic implications of corporate financial reporting," *Journal of Accounting and Economics*, Vol. 40, Nos. 1–3, pp. 3–73.

Hsu, P., X. Tian, and Y. Xu (2014), "Financial development and innovation: Cross-country evidence," *Journal of Financial Economics*, Vol. 112, No. 1, pp. 116–135.

Jibril, H., A. Kaltenbrunner, and E. Kesidou (2018), "Financialization and innovation in emerging economies: Evidence from Brazil," *Leeds University Business School Working Paper*, No. 18–09.

Kaplan, S. N. and B. A. Minton (2012), "How has CEO turnover changed?" *International Review of Finance*, Vol. 12, No. 1, pp. 57–87.

Kerr, W. and R. Nanda (2015), "Financing innovation," *Annual Review of Financial Economics*, Vol. 7, No. 1, pp. 445–462.

Lazonick, W. and M. O'Sullivan (2000), "Maximization shareholder value: A new ideology for corporate governance," *Economy and Society*, Vol. 29, No. 1, pp. 13–35.

Lee, Y. S., H. S. Kim, and H. J. Seo (2020), "Financialization and innovation short-termism in OECD countries," *Review of Radical Political Economics*, Vol. 52, No. 2, pp. 259–286.

Narayanan, M. P. (1985), "Managerial incentives for short-term results," *Journal of Finance*, Vol. 40, No. 5, pp. 1469–1484.

Orhangazi, Ö. (2008), "Financialization and capital accumulation in the nonfinancial corporate sector: A theoretical and empirical investigation of the US economy, 1973–2004," *Cambridge Journal of Economics*, Vol. 32, No. 6, pp. 863–886.

Pellegrino, G. and M. Savona (2017), "No money, no honey? Financial versus knowledge and demand constraints on innovation," *Research Policy*, Vol. 46, No. 2, pp. 510–521.

Porter, M. E. (1992), "Capital disadvantage: America's falling capital investment system," *Harvard Business Review*, Vol. 70, No. 5, pp. 65–82.

Seo, H. J., S. J. Kang, and Y. J. Baek (2020), "Managerial myopia and short-termism of innovation strategy: Financialization of Korean firms," *Cambridge Journal of Economics*, Vol. 44, No. 6, pp. 1197–1220.

Seo, H. J., H. S. Kim, and Y. C. Kim (2012), "Financialization and the slow-down in Korean firms' R&D investment," *Asian Economic Papers*, Vol. 11, No. 3, pp. 35–49.

Stein, J. C. (1988), "Takeover threats and managerial myopia," *Journal of Political Economy*, Vol. 96, No. 1, pp. 61–80.

Stein, J. C. (1989), "Efficient capital markets, inefficient firms: A model of myopic corporation behavior," *Quarterly Journal of Economics*, Vol. 104, No. 4, pp. 655–669.

Stockhammer, E. (2004), "Financialisation and the slowdown of accumulation," *Cambridge Journal of Economics*, Vol. 28, No. 5, pp. 719–741.

Stockhammer, E. (2008), "Stylized facts on the finance-dominated accumulation regime," *Competition and Change*, Vol. 12, No. 2, pp. 189–207.

Stout, L. (2012), *The shareholder value myth*, San Francisco: Berrett-Koehler Publishers.

Database

OECD database (https://data.oecd.org/, retrieved on October 10, 2021).

2 Financialization and corporate innovation strategy

The financialization concept provides a useful framework for understanding and analyzing the global financial crisis of 2008 and the growing influence of finance on society overall. Academic interest and debate over the past 30 years have focused on theoretical discussion about the definition of financialization and on empirical studies measuring economic changes—and the scale of those changes—caused by financialization. The theoretical discussion deals with how to encompass within the definition of financialization the various phenomena through which finance intersects with the interests of households, businesses, industries, national economies, and the global economy.

This research also considers how financialization has changed corporate governance priorities through the principles of maximizing shareholder value. Following the outbreak of the 2008 financial crisis, theoretical discussion of financialization has also come to address the correlation between financialization and the causes of the crisis. Seeking to apply and support theoretical perspectives, empirical studies analyze the trends and content of the various structural changes caused by financialization. These studies have developed various indicators to quantitatively measure financialization and analyze the correlation between financialization and various macroeconomic changes (sluggish real investment, job instability, increased income inequality, outbreaks of financial crises, etc.).

What does financialization mean?

Kevin Philips first used the term *financialization* in his book *Boiling Point* (1993), and further discussed the term in *Arrogant Capital* a year later. One chapter of the second book looks in-depth at financialization in the United States. In this chapter, Philips indicates that the long-term separation of the real economy and the financial economy is a hallmark

DOI: 10.4324/9781003240822-2

of the financialization process. The definition of financialization used in more recent research has diverged somewhat from the Phillips definition, coming to broadly encompass the new economic phenomena emerging at various economic levels since the 1980s.

First, at the household level, Aglietta (2000) connects financialization to the increasing relative importance of financial income over earned income in household consumption and savings decisions. Second, at the corporate level, Froud et al. (2000), Williams (2000), Lazonick and O'Sullivan (2000), Aglietta (2000), and Aglietta and Rebérioux (2005) employ the concept of financialization to describe the emergence of a corporate governance outlook that seeks to maximize shareholder value. Third, at the industry level, Phillips (2002) and Krippner (2005) define financialization in terms of the increasing importance of the financial industry relative to non-financial industries in a country's employment and value-added production processes. Fourth, Boyer (2000), Duménil and Lévy (2004), and Epstein and Jayadev (2005) use the term financialization in macroeconomic analyses. In sum, these authors interpret financialization as an accumulation regime in which the financial system is at the peak of the institutional hierarchy or serves as a stage in capitalist economic development in which the economic and political power of the financial elites and rent-seeking classes expand according to the tradition of Hilferding (Crotty, 2005; Epstein and Javadev, 2005). In particular, post-Keynesians such as Stockhammer (2004) and Orhangazi (2008) analyze the macroeconomic effects of financialization, namely the negative effects of financialization on production, employment, and investment. Finally, Eatwell and Taylor (2002) and Phillips (1994) also define financialization within the context of the explosive increase in international financial transactions in the global economy.

As described above, financialization refers in aggregate to the new economic phenomena arising from the increasing importance of financial markets, financial motives, financial institutions, and financial elites in the operation of the economy and its governing institutions, both at the national and international levels, these trends having emerged mainly since the 1980s.

Previous discussions on financialization are summarized in Table 2.1. In the table, "Expansion of financialization" refers to the process in which the realm of financialization gradually expands from the corporate unit to the global economy, while "Development of financialization" summarizes the various social and economic consequences of financialization. Thus, "Expansion of financialization" proceeds from the level of the corporation to the household, industry,

Table 2.1 Prior research on financialization

Development of financialization \ Expansion of financialization	Corporation	Household	Industry	National economy	Global economy
Formation of norms and principles	Shareholder primacy	Penetration of financial norms into consumption norms (increasing relative importance of financial income over earned income in consumption and saving decisions).	Primacy of the financial sector over the non-financial sector through financing, valuation, and restructuring.	Financial system at the top of the institutional hierarchy. Financial norms limit other institutional forms, resulting in institutional transformation.	Globalized dominance of financial norms.
Momentum for the formation of norms	Need to escape from the crisis of Fordism	Demographic changes, financial deregulation, moderate wage income increases.	Capital moved into the financial sector as the rate of return on financial assets began to rise above the rate of return on real investment in the late 1970s due to high interest rates and greater financial liberalization.	Need to escape from the crisis of Fordism.	Globalization.

(continued)

Table 2.1 Cont.

Expansion of financialization / Development of financialization	Corporation	Household	Industry	National economy	Global economy
Strategies and policies	Corporate strategies to maximize shareholder value: downsizing, mergers and acquisitions, value chain reengineering, greater employment flexibility, stock buybacks.	Household consumption and savings decisions are influenced by collective management of savings by institutional investors, portfolio management aimed at maximizing financial returns, and expected financial returns. As a result, of financial assets owned by households, the proportion of low-yield	Financial institutions develop mechanisms and means to induce non-financial companies to act in accordance with financial norms, doing so through corporate credit ratings and development of new financial techniques and financial products.	(1) Industrial relations: Industrial relations has been a primary victim of pressures to increase the rate of return as companies have introduced a variety of so-called "flexible employment strategies." (2) Competition: The arena of competition has moved from the product market to the financial market.	Implementation of economic policies promoting globalization of finance (Washington Consensus), formation of a single global capital market (As borders have opened, market segmentation within national markets has weakened. This means that within individual national markets, divisions and

deposits dropped while holdings of financial assets with high, long-term expected returns increased. Thus, there was a gradual shift of household interest from short-term liquidity to long-term asset management.

(3) State: Government expenditures have become more sensitive to the real interest rate on market-traded government bonds, and this has limited government debt levels.

(4) Global economy: Deregulation and liberalization have led to financial norms at a global level.

boundaries between the currency market, financial market, foreign exchange market, and futures market have disappeared. Investors seek to maximize profit by moving freely from stocks of one company to stocks of another, from one country's currency to another, and from corporate bonds to government bonds.)

(continued)

Table 2.1 Cont.

Development of financialization \ Expansion of financialization		Corporation	Household	Industry	National economy	Global economy
Economic effects	Income distribution	Income distribution favorable to shareholders and managers, with a widening wage gap between managers and workers.	Expanded income inequality between households due to increased disparity between property income and wage income.	Transfer of income from the non-financial sector to the financial sector. (The non-financial sector pays increasingly more in interest and dividends to the financial sector.)	Expanded share of interest and dividend income in national income.	Financial wealth concentrated in three centers: USA, Europe, and Japan.
	Other effects	Low investment and stagnant employment gains despite recovery in corporate profits.	Increased household debt.	Predominance of funding through the stock market, rather than through banks. Growing economic importance of the FIRE (finance, insurance, and real estate) sector in terms of employment and value-added creation.	(1) Consumption: Consumption has been a driver of growth due to easy household access to credit. But higher household debt promotes systemic instability. (2) Investment: Adherence to	Foreign exchange transactions in financial assets overshadow foreign exchange transactions related to international trade in goods and services.

(continued)

the goal of maximizing shareholder value leads to subdued investment, with corporate profits having been decoupled from investment.

(3) Financial market deregulation facilitates the free movement of capital. This leads to rapid exchange rate fluctuations, a factor of uncertainty that leads to repeated financial crises. (4) Although the share of government expenditure to GDP remains stable, still-high government

Table 2.1 Cont.

Expansion of financialization / Development of financialization	Corporation	Household	Industry	National economy	Global economy
	Dividend payout ratio, EVA (economic value added), interest and dividend payments to the financial sector by the non-financial sector, the proportion			expenditures contribute to economic stability. (5) Macroeconomic performance is characterized by low aggregate demand growth and high system instability.	
Economic indicators of financialization		Ratio of household financial assets to household total assets.	Share of employment in the FIRE sector and share of total economic value-added production by the FIRE sector.	Share of interest and dividend income to GDP.	International financial transactions as a percentage of global GDP.

	of financial assets in the non-financial sector.				
Studies	Froud et al. (2000), Williams (2000), Lazonick & O'Sullivan (2000), Aglietta (2000), Aglietta & Rebérioux (2005)	Aglietta (2000)	Phillips (2002), Orhangazi (2008), Kus (2012), Darcillon (2015)	Boyer (2000), Duménil and Lévy (2004), Epstein and Jayadev (2005), Stockhammer (2004), Orhangazi (2008)	Eatwell & Taylor (2002), Phillips (1994)

national economy, and global economy, and the columns of the table correspond to corporate financialization, household financialization,[1] industrial financialization,[2] growth regime financialization (national economy),[3] and international transaction financialization (global economy).[4] Likewise, the individual rows of the table for "Development of financialization" address the formation of financial norms and principles, momentum for the formation of norms, strategies, and policies for realizing norms, and the economic consequences of norms (income distribution and other economic effects). Of the above forms of financialization, this book focuses on the results of prior research into financialization that are directly related to the technological innovation activities of companies.

Corporate financialization

Emergence of shareholder value management

The social compromises between companies and workers that led to the post-World War II golden age in the United States and other advanced countries began to erode in the 1980s with intensified domestic and international competition and the advent of the shareholder value model. During the so-called Fordist period (the years after World War II), workers were given job security, and were also guaranteed a stable income with wage levels linked to productivity improvements. In addition, workers engaged in collective bargaining with firms to jointly determine rules on various aspects of employment relations, such as working conditions and wages. However, with the emergence of newly industrialized countries in the late 1970s, competition in advanced nations between domestic and foreign companies intensified, and company profitability declined. As a result, the social contract between companies and workers came under pressure.

In the 1980s, corporate management principles emphasizing shareholder primacy rapidly gained wide acceptance, and various labor flexibility and financial strategies were adopted to maximize shareholder wealth. Due to these environmental changes, an important virtuous cycle—which had been buttressed by the consensus between companies and workers—ceased to function properly. Historically, productivity improvements had led to wage increases, and these wage increases became the basis for mass consumption. Rising domestic demand then promoted further investment, with that higher investment bringing about yet more productivity gains. However, this cycle of growth, which was observed during the Fordist period, broke down for the reasons mentioned above.

The OECD (1998) summarizes the changes as follows:

> One of the most significant structural changes in the economies of OECD countries in the 1980s and 1990s has been the emergence of increasingly efficient markets in corporate control and an attendant rise in shareholders' capability to influence management of publicly held companies. In particular, owing to the expanded possibilities for investors to use the capital market to measure and compare corporate performance of corporations and to discipline corporate management, the commitment of management to producing shareholder value has become perceptibly stronger; this represents a significant change in the behavior of large corporations.
>
> (OECD, 1998: p. 15)

In most developed countries under the Fordist paradigm after the Great Depression, the roles and influence of shareholders in companies were limited. This was the result of laws clearly separating the real and financial sectors and reducing the role of the financial sector in the economy, doing so to prevent financial crises from spreading to the real sector. Financial transactions and capital flows were controlled, and limits were placed on interest rates. Under these conditions, shareholders could only exercise limited influence on decision-making by managers. However, as circumstances evolved in the 1970s, financial liberalization and the opening of the financial market led to the development of new financial products and instruments. Notably, junk bonds and high-risk/high-yield securities were leveraged in hostile takeovers to gain control of companies. This helped establish the market for corporate control. Shareholders now exert influence over companies more effectively through the threat of replacing under-performing managers. Professor Berle of Columbia University and Professor Dodd of Harvard University began the debate about the fundamentals of corporate goals, with their positions being articulated in the *Harvard Law Review* in 1932. Berle—one of the authors of *The Modern Corporation and Private Property* (1932), the first book on modern corporate governance—supported shareholder primacy, insisting that the authority bestowed to corporations and managers must be exercised only for the benefit of shareholders. Taking the opposite view, Professor Dodd argued that the firm should not only earn profits for shareholders but must also seek to create stable jobs, produce high-quality products for consumers, and contribute to society. In the 1970s, the Berle position on the primacy of shareholder value was promoted again through adherents to the Chicago school of economics. Most famously, Milton Friedman asserted in the *New York Times* in 1970 that since shareholders are the owners of the company, the sole social responsibility of a company is to maximize profits for its shareholders. Six years later, Jensen and Meckling (1976) defined shareholders as the principals with authority to hire managers and defined managers as agents of the shareholders. The legitimacy of shareholder value management was explained in the context of the principal agent problem. Separation of ownership and management incurs agency costs (monitoring costs, bonding costs, and residual costs) due to opportunistic behavior by managers. As a result, autonomous management by managers leads to waste. Therefore, stricter control over agents (managers) by owners (shareholders) should improve company efficiency and maximize company value.

The term "shareholder value management" is now widely used in the media (including newspapers and broadcasters), as well as in academia, and the principles of maximization of shareholder value have become the norm in boardrooms around the world. As a result, stakeholder management, the dominant paradigm of the past that sought to protect the interests of workers and other stakeholders, is now criticized for encouraging opportunistic behavior by managers chasing their own goals (building reputation, securing social influence, etc.) at the expense of shareholder interest (Stout, 2012). Today, to maximize shareholder value, companies adopt new strategies that focus on labor flexibility, corporate value-chain rationalization, leverage effects, stock repurchases, and investment in financial assets rather than real assets.

Shareholder value maximization and corporate financialization

Corporate financialization is a direct result of the principle of shareholder value maximization. In the 1980s, many changes took place in corporate governance. As Lazonick and O'Sullivan (2000) explain, the core business management principles prior to the 1980s could be summed up as "retain" and "reinvest." These emphasize employment stability and investment in real and human capital. However, maximizing shareholder value became the overriding goal of corporate governance in the 1908s. Likewise, "downsizing" and "distributions" have replaced "retain" and "reinvest" as guiding keywords for managers today. Shareholder wealth is promoted through major corporate restructuring and downsizing. Dividends to shareholders are increased at the expense of reinvesting those funds internally in equipment and machinery. With the trend toward managing for shareholder value, mergers and acquisitions, reengineering of the value chain, and stock buybacks have all been integrated more deeply into corporate strategy. Companies have also adopted flexible labor policies to improve short-term rates of return.

With more ways to hire workers, the proportion of non-regular workers, such as part-time and contract workers, has also swelled. As more and more employees are hired through individual contracts, collective bargaining, and standard contract practices of the Fordist period have been substantially neutralized. The inexorable decline in union membership can be understood in this context. As Wallerstein (1999) points out, modern management trends have pushed up income inequality. Aglietta and Rebérioux (2005) explain the correlation between shareholder value management and labor flexibility using the indicator of economic value added (EVA).

They find that shareholders evaluate managerial performance using EVA more than with traditional measures, such as net income. One strategy for raising EVA is to introduce greater flexibility into employment and wages. Adoption of various labor flexibility strategies has led to an income distribution favoring shareholders and managers. This structure that disadvantages labor over capital is the result of de-indexation of wage to productivity and high dividend payouts (Lazonick and O'Sullivan, 2000; Boyer, 2000).

Dividend payout and EVA are major indicators of corporate financialization. As seen in Figure 2.1., the dividend payout ratio in the United States has increased by about 2.7 times over the past 30 years, from 30% (1979), to 125% (2001) and 79% (2008).

Aglietta and Rebérioux (2005) suggest that EVA is the indicator that best reflects the principle of shareholder value management. Under EVA, cost of capital is an explicit opportunity cost and the realization of profit above the investor's capital cost is the goal of corporate financial activities. EVA is further linked to the maximization of shareholder value because residual profit (calculated by deducting the company's capital cost from operating profit) is vested to shareholders. Stockhammer (2004), Crotty (2005), Duménil and Lévy (2000), and Aglietta and Breton (2001) assert that the emergence of management principles emphasizing shareholder value has led to managerial myopia and that this myopia is the cause of depressed investment in tangible and intangible assets. In other words, managers obliged to focus on short-term performance by emphasizing shareholder value must sacrifice the long term for the short term in their decisions on production, investment, and finance.

Managers thus prefer to invest in small, incremental improvements rather than in large, long-term investments, such as R&D, and they use

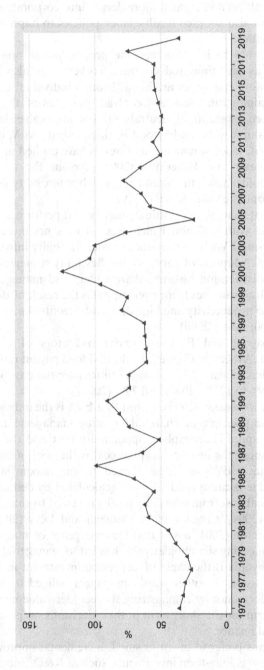

Figure 2.1 Dividend payout ratio of US non-financial companies.
Source: Flow of Funds (Table F. 102).

net profit that would otherwise have been invested in tangible and intangible assets to purchase financial assets, pay dividends, and buy back treasury stock. Figure 2.2 depicts the ratio of financial assets to total assets, showing the extent to which US non-financial companies have increased their investments in financial assets relative to investments in real assets. The ratio of financial assets to total assets by US non-financial institutions rose from 27.8% in 1975 to 47.5% in 2019. Growing by 1.7 times over the past 45 years, this percentage peaked in 2009 at 52.3%. In addition, underinvestment in R&D and equipment due to the pressures of shareholder value management threatens corporate competitiveness and firm value over the long term. As shown in Figure 2.3, growth of US non-financial company investment in non-residential structures has gradually decreased since the 1970s. Having reached 12% in the early 1980s, the investment growth rate rapidly dropped to 6% in the early 1990s, and currently sits at 3.8% (2021).

Economic effects of corporate financialization

A significant portion of studies into the economic effects of corporate financialization investigate the correlation between corporate investment sluggishness and financialization. Stockhammer (2004 and 2005), Crotty (2005), Duménil and Lévy (2000), Orhangazi (2008), and Demir (2009) empirically analyze the link between lethargic investment and financialization in the United States and other advanced countries. These authors also link financialization to low corporate investment in Turkey and South America, places experiencing frequent financial crises. Seo et al. (2012) and Seo et al. (2016) analyze the correlation between financialization and weak investment by Korean companies.

Another area of research deals with the impact of financialization on employment and the labor market. Related studies focus on relationships between the following: financialization and poor employment growth (Lin, 2016), financialization and labor market flexibility (Darcillon, 2015; Seo et al., 2015), and financialization and functional income distribution (Stockhammer, 2009; Sjöberg, 2009; Onaran, Stockhammer and Grafl, 2011; Kus, 2012). In addition, Stockhammer (2009), Tridico (2012), and Boyer (2013) consider the relationship between financialization and financial crises, especially the 2008 global financial crisis. Finally, in recent years, Régulation theory (Boyer, 2000; Aglietta and Breton, 2001) and post-Keynesian economics (Stockhammer, 2004 and 2005; Hein, 2014) have served as frameworks to model financialization. In particular, the latter presents a financialization model based on the stock-flow model (Skott and Ryoo, 2008).

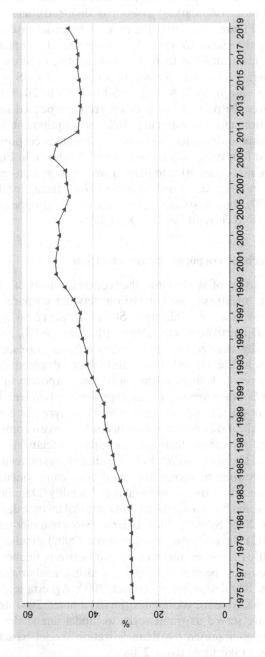

Figure 2.2 Ratio of financial assets to total assets of US non-financial companies.

Source: Flow of Funds (Table B. 103).

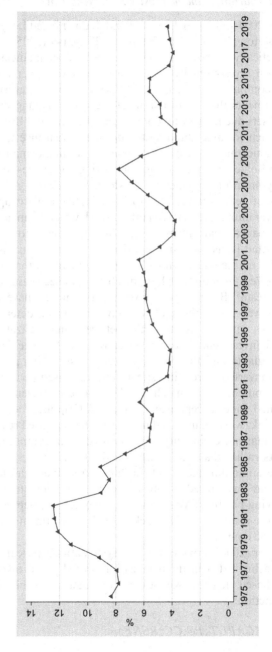

Figure 2.3 Growth rate of investment in nonresidential structures of US non-financial companies.

Source: Flow of Funds (Table B. 103).

Corporate financialization and lackluster real investment

Stockhammer (2004 and 2005), Crotty (2005), Duménil and Lévy (2004), Aglietta and Breton (2001), Boyer (2000), and Krippner (2005) use modelling to theoretically analyze potential linkages between financialization and lagging real investment by firms. Crotty and Krippner note that non-financial companies in the United States earn better returns from financial investments than from real assets, leading to sluggish investment in real assets due to crowding out effects. Aglietta and Breton take another approach to understanding the decline in real investment. As shareholder value management has come to dominate management thinking, shareholders are increasingly pressuring companies to pull up share prices by promoting dividends and stock repurchases. As a result, the proportion of net profit allocated to real investment has dropped.

Finally, Boyer illuminates a third path through which financialization negatively impacts real investment. As financial norms have transformed—that is, as the minimum desired rate of return required by the financial markets has climbed—investment plans that are relatively risky and require long time horizons have also been cancelled and delayed. As a result, Boyer argues, investment strategies have become more conservative, even as the quality of investments has deteriorated.

These studies into the relationship between financialization and restrained real investment focus on three main links. The first link, proposed by Aglietta and Breton, is between the shrinking proportion of net profit converted to real investment and increased dividends and treasury stock purchases as the shareholder value management viewpoint has gained wider acceptance. Crotty and Krippner focus on the crowding out link, wherein financial investment has replaced real investment as non-financial companies have boosted their commitments to financial assets rather than real assets. Lastly, Boyer suggests that the increase in the minimum rate of return that shareholders and financial markets demand has caused companies to suspend investments that risk not achieving positive EVAs. This link suggests that depressed real investment is the result of scaling back high-risk investments requiring patience over the long term.

Stockhammer (2004) provides the first systematic empirical analysis of the relationship between financialization and sluggish investment. This analysis, based on a post-Keynesian model, estimates the following investment function:

$$ACCU = f\left(CAPUT, PS, CC; RSNF\right) \tag{2.1}$$

where ACCU, CAPUT, PS, CC, and RSNF represent investment, capacity utilization, profit share, relative cost of capital, and rentiers' share of non-financial business, respectively.

Stockhammer uses OECD data to examine the effects of financialization on real investment in the United States (1963–1997), the United Kingdom (1970–1996), France (1978–1997), and Germany (1963–1990). This analysis focuses on the Crotty and Krippner link between financialization and real investment, defining financialization as interest and dividend income earned by non-financial businesses divided by the total value added by those businesses. Investment is defined as the growth rate of gross business capital stock. The study confirms the negative effect of financialization on accumulation in the United States, the UK, and France. Notably, financialization accounts for most of the drop in real investment in France, and a third of the decline in the United States. On the other hand, the study results on the connection between financialization and real investment in Germany are unclear. According to Stockhammer, that is because the level of financialization in Germany is relatively low compared to that of the United Kingdom, France, and the United States. Orhangazi (2008) analyzes the correlation between financialization and real investment using GMM modelling to control for endogeneity in US company data between 1973 and 2003. This analysis considers two of the links mentioned above: Aglietta and Breton link of higher interest and dividend payments by non-financial firms to the financial markets, reducing available internal funds available for real investment; and the Crotty and Krippner link of financial assets crowding out real investment.

Orhangazi looks at financialization trends using US macro data from 1952 to 2003 to consider (1) whether non-financial companies ramped up investments in financial assets, (2) whether non-financial companies added to their income through investments in financial assets, (3) whether non-financial companies paid out more in interest and dividend payments to financial markets, and (4) whether real investment declined over the long term. The results show that non-financial company investment in financial assets, income from financial asset investment, and interest and dividends to the financial markets increased in the 1970s, whereas investment in real assets diminished during that decade. Having confirmed the long-term financialization trend, Orhangazi sets up the following investment equation for GMM estimation.

$$\frac{I}{K} = f\left(\frac{\pi}{K}, \frac{S}{K}, \frac{D}{K}, \frac{P}{K}, \frac{\pi^f}{K}\right) \tag{2.2}$$

where K is capital stock, I is real investment, π is profit, S is sales, D is long-term debt, P is payments to the financial market, and is π^f is income from investments in financial assets.

The $\dfrac{P}{K}$ and $\dfrac{\pi^f}{K}$ variables correspond to the Aglietta and Breton link and the Crotty and Krippner link, respectively. This estimation confirms that financialization has had a negative impact on corporate investment. When estimating the impact by firm size and industry, the Aglietta and Breton link is found to be valid regardless of industry and firm size, while the Crotty and Krippner link shows up more clearly among large firms.

Davis (2018) also explores the correlation between financialization and real investment, doing so using US company data from 1971 to 2011. The difference between the Orhangazi and Davis studies is that the latter more explicitly considers the following two variables: (1) norms of shareholder value management and (2) uncertainty and volatility of the business environment.

Davis proposes the following estimation equation:

$$\frac{I}{K} = f\left(u, \pi, i^{\text{dep}}, i^{\text{debt}}, M, D; SV, V\right) \tag{2.3}$$

where I is investment, K is capital stock, u is utilization rate, π is profit rate, i^{dep} is return on investment on financial assets, i^{debt} is interest payment on debt, M is financial assets, D is debt, SV is shareholder value management norm, and V is uncertainty in the business environment, respectively.

In this study, stock repurchases and the standard deviation of capital stock to sales are included as proxies for the norms of stockholder value management (a distinct feature of the above estimation equation) and uncertainty in the business environment, respectively. Davis confirms that the norms of shareholder value management and uncertainty in the business environment led to a dwindling of real investment by non-financial companies in the United States. However, the results differ by company size: norms of shareholder value management exhibit a negative effect on real investment by large corporations, while uncertainty in the business environment drags down real investment by SMEs.

Impact of corporate financialization on subdued employment and on labor market flexibility

As Lazonick and O'Sullivan (2000) emphasize, corporate management has been increasingly dominated by short-termism in recent years. Companies undergoing major restructuring and downsizing to maximize shareholder value have not invested in human capital to enhance their core competencies and competitiveness over the long-term. While many theoretical studies have explored the relationship between financialization and the labor market, relatively few empirical studies have done the same (Lin, 2016).

Lin (2016) presents the systematic investigation into the correlation between financialization and static employment, doing so using firm-level data. This panel analysis looks at S&P Compustat data between 1982 and 2005 to identify how financialization has affected employment in US non-financial firms. For the analysis, 957 companies were selected (of the 17,673 companies in the Fortune 500, only those that had been in the index for at least five years). Lin estimates employment effects for three categories of jobs: professional and managerial, blue-collar, and service. Thus, the study not only estimates the impact of financialization on overall employment but also compares and analyzes how financialization has impacted these individual employment categories.

Lin measures corporate financialization using three variables: investment in financial assets (ratio of financial assets to total assets), debt ratio (total liabilities to total assets), and compensation to shareholders (sum of stock repurchases and dividends relative to total expenditures). Based on the reasoning that aggressive investment in financial assets has dampened employment by leaving fewer resources available for growth through hiring, investment in financial assets serves as a proxy for corporate financialization. The decision to use the debt-to-equity ratio assumes that growing interest payments on higher debt holds back employment. Finally, shareholder compensation represents the returns from restructuring and downsizing implemented to maximize shareholder returns, assumed to come at the cost of holding and reinvesting fewer past earnings.

Lin finds that all three variables—investment in financial assets, debt ratio, and compensation to shareholders—are statistically significant causes of sluggish employment in US firms, with compensation for shareholders having the strongest impact of the three. Investment in financial assets increased employment of professionals and managers and of service workers but had a negative impact on blue-collar hiring. Further, this negative effect of financialization on employment was higher on blue-collar workers than the positive effects on the other employment categories, and the negative effects are found to have intensified over time.

Darcillon (2015) systematically analyzes the relationship between financialization and the labor market. This empirical analysis of data from 16 OECD countries between 1970 and 2009 finds that financialization weakened worker bargaining power and increased labor flexibility. The author reports that globalization and the opening of financial markets eroded the bargaining power of labor relative to capital, which reduced the benefits of belonging to a trade union and lead to a gradual decline in union membership.

Accordingly, as employment decisions are now made on an individual—rather than a collective—basis, the bargaining power of workers has further dissipated. In addition, as shareholder value management became the dominant outlook in corporate boardrooms, companies have adopted labor flexibility strategies to further improve short-term returns. Individual employment contracts have become the norm, doing so at the expense of group contracts negotiated through collective bargaining, and this has resulted in greater diversity between the contracts and wage levels of individual workers. Finally, the proportion of contract-based and other non-regular workers has also swelled.

To analyze the impact of financialization on labor relations, Darcillon presents the following estimation equation:

$$Y = \alpha_i + \beta_1 Fin + \sum_{k=1}^{n} \beta_k X_k + \epsilon \qquad (2.4)$$

Where, Y, Fin and X are variables representing bargaining power of labor (or degree of employment protection), financialization-related variables, and control variables, respectively.

This study estimates the degree of worker bargaining power in individual countries based on a three-factor worker bargaining power model. Darcillon posits that bargaining power is determined by union membership rate (ud), the compulsory application rate of collective bargaining (ext), and the degree of collective bargaining in wage settings ($wcoord$):
$bargaining = 0.1159 ud_{i,t} + 0.4560 ext_{i,t} + 0.4299 wcoord_{i,t}$.

Employment protection is measured using an OECD-developed index. The share of the financial sector within total value-added production and the share of employment in the financial sector represent the degree of financialization. The analysis finds that worker bargaining power retreats as financialization (under both variables used in the study) progresses and as trade (a control variable) is liberalized. In the analysis of the correlation between employment protection and financialization, both financialization variables weakened employment protection, meaning that financialization promotes labor flexibility. Progress in trade liberalization and a high unemployment rate (control variables) are found to weaken employment protection as well.

Seo et al. (2015) use the Rodrik (1997) model to analyze how financialization and changes in corporate governance have influenced employment and wage decisions by Korean companies, suggesting that shareholder value management impacts employment in two ways.

The authors assume the following labor demand function:

$$lnN_{i,t} = \theta_0 + \theta_1 \ln\left(\frac{w_i}{c}\right) + \theta_2 lnQ_{i,t} + \theta_3 lnA_{i,t} \tag{2.5}$$

where Q, K, N, A, t, w, and c represent value-added, capital stock, employment, technology efficiency, time, wages, and user cost of capital, respectively.

This equation implies two potential channels through which shareholder value prioritization may affect employment.

First, companies adhering to shareholder value management principles prefer higher efficiency over new employment. As a result, these firms adopt labor-saving technologies or make greater use of outsourcing to raise the static efficiency of internal operations. Thus, shareholder value management targets technological change or efficiency improvements, which ultimately lead to lower employment.

$$A_{i,t} = e^{\delta_0 T_i} F_{i,t}^{\delta_1}, \delta_0 \text{ and } \delta_1 > 0 \tag{2.6}$$

where T and F represent the time trend and the degree of financialization, respectively.

Substituting equation (2.6) into equation (2.5) and adding an error term yields the following labor demand function to be estimated.

$$\ln N_{i,t} = \theta_0 + \theta_4 T + \theta_1 \ln\left(\frac{w_i}{c}\right) + \theta_2 lnQ_{i,t} + \theta_5 lnF_{i,t} + \eta_{i,t} \tag{2.7}$$

where $\theta_4 = \theta_3\delta_0$ and $\theta_5 = \delta_1\theta_3$. And $\eta_{i,t}$ is an error term.

In equation (2.7), if the efficiency enhancements induced by shareholder value management works, $\theta_5 < 0$.

The second channel through which financialization may determine employment conditions is by increasing the elasticity of labor demand. As companies yield to the pressures of shareholder value management, they adopt new labor-saving technologies and make greater use of outsourcing at home and abroad. This raises the likelihood that domestic labor will be replaced by other domestic and foreign inputs. As a result, the elasticity of labor demand increases. In equation (2.5), θ_1 is the degree of elasticity of labor demand to wages, a function of shareholder value management. In other words, as indicated above, as the opportunities to substitute labor with other inputs grows under the mainstreaming of the shareholder value management outlook, the degree of elasticity also increases: $\theta_1 = \kappa_0 + \kappa_1 F_{i,t}$. Unlike in equation (2.6), equation (2.5) only assumes exogenous technological improvements: $A_{i,t} = e^{\delta_0 T_i}$.

Thus, equation (2.5) is expressed as follows.

$$\ln N_{i,t} = \theta_0 + \theta_T T_i + \kappa_0 \ln\left(\frac{w_i}{c}\right) + \kappa_1 \left[\ln\left(\frac{w_i}{c}\right)\right] F_{i,t} + \theta_2 \ln Q_{i,t} + \eta_{i,t} \quad (2.8)$$

where $\theta_T = \delta_0 \theta_3$. $\kappa_1 < 0$ indicates that shareholder value management has made labor demand more elastic.

Seo et al. (2015) next examine the impact of shareholder value management on wages:

$$\ln w_{i,t} = \beta_0 + \beta_1 \ln q_{i,t} + \beta_2 \ln N_{i,t} + \beta_3 \ln X_{i,t} + \epsilon_{i,t} \quad (2.9)$$

Equation (2.9) is fundamentally based on the collective bargaining and efficiency wage models.

q represents value added per worker, a variable reflecting rent-sharing under the collective bargaining model. Alternatively, q can represent the degree to which wages are linked to productivity improvements, as discussed under Régulation theory. N, which represents the level of employment of a company, controls for the fact that larger companies pay relatively higher wages. As a monopsony model assumes, firms pay higher wages as they increase the size of their organization (Konings and Vandebussche, 1995). X stands for other variables that influence the wage level of a company, which in this context reflects the impact of shareholder value management or financialization.

Seo et al. (2015) use KISVALUE data for 2000–2010 to analyze the impact of financialization and a stronger shareholder value management outlook (represented by EVA and ROE [return on equity]) on employment and wages in Korea.

The estimation results are summarized as follows. First, maximizing shareholder value had a negative effect on employment. However, the study did not clearly confirm that lower employment was brought about by efficiency improvements induced by shareholder value management (the first channel described above). Also, based on the Rodrik hypothesis, the study looked at whether wage elasticity of labor demand propped up by shareholder value management suppressed employment.

The estimation results confirmed that the increase in labor demand elasticity was not only the result of globalization (as suggested by Rodrik) but also the result of financialization, especially financialization induced by shareholder value management. Therefore, a more flexible labor demand curve for Korean companies means that fluctuations in employment brought about by external shocks are greater than if the labor demand curve were more inelastic. For example, external shocks such as the 2008 global financial crisis are likely to result in a larger drop in demand for Korean products—as well as have a great negative impact on employment—than such shocks would have had in the past. Second, the equation (2.9) estimates confirm that stricter adherence to the shareholder value management perspective negatively affects wage formation.

Corporate financialization and innovation

We have reviewed the results of various theoretical and empirical studies showing the negative impact of financialization on real investment (Boyer 2000; Duménil and Lévy, 2000; Aglietta and Breton, 2001; Stockhammer, 2004 and 2005; Crotty, 2005; Krippner, 2005). In a similar vein, other research analyzes how financialization affects investment in intangible assets, especially R&D. Seo, Kim, and Kim (2012) use Korean firm data (1994–2009) to analyze the impact of a stronger shareholder value orientation on R&D investment by Korean firms, reaching the following conclusions.

First, higher dividend payouts and stock repurchases have reduced R&D investment, and favorable investment and investment opportunities in financial assets have crowded out R&D investment. Second, looking separately at the periods before and after the 1997 Asian financial crisis, advances in financialization negatively impacted R&D investment only over the latter period. These results demonstrate that R&D investment by Korean firms contracted as financialization progressed, and that the negative effects of financialization rose after 1997. In a similar study, Jibril, Kaltenbrunner, and Kesidou (2018) analyze the impact of financialization on corporate innovation, as measured by intangible assets, for 94 Brazilian manufacturers during the 2011–2016 period. These authors find that, while financial liabilities do not affect investment in intangibles, higher levels of financial assets and profits discourage investment in intangibles. However, the results of this analysis are not clear on what effect dividends and stock repurchases have on intangible asset investment. The authors conclude that increasing financial asset purchases by Brazilian firms resulting from better financial opportunities crowd out investments in intangible assets.

While above studies consider the effect of financialization on R&D investment, other research looks at the impact of financialization on technological innovation strategies. The current study is primarily focused on this link between financialization and technological innovation strategies. An empirical study of US firms by Edmans, Fang, and Lewellen (2017) finds that managerial myopia reduced real investment and budgets for short-term R&D projects.

As M&A-related threats emerge and impatient stockholder behavior comes to dominate, and as stock prices serve as stronger signals of managerial competence, managers are forced to focus more on short-term profitability and stock price management than on long-term corporate competitiveness. Thus, managers are driven to withdraw from long-term R&D projects or reduce investments in radical innovation that negatively affect short-term performance, even if such projects or investments would have promoted long-term corporate value. In this process, these same managers increase investments in financial assets and restructure and promote corporate flexibility to enhance short-term corporate returns.

Lee et al. (2020) analyze how financialization has affected technological innovation strategies in OECD countries and conclude that, as managerial myopia worsens in line with deepening financialization, economic entities direct technological innovation strategies toward incremental innovation at the expense of radical innovation, which involves high-risk and long-term investment. Specifically, using macroeconomic data from 31 OECD countries (1990–2006) to study the relationship between financialization and innovation short-termism, Lee et al. (2020) find that advancing financialization was followed by declining radicalness of technological innovation and a higher number of patent registrations. Significantly, this is the first study to directly consider the relationship between financialization and innovation short-termism.

The above research results confirm that financialization has a negative effect on technological innovation by reducing R&D investment and promoting short-termism of innovation strategy. However, though empirical studies find reduced R&D investment, the number of patent registrations, another quantitative indicator of innovation performance, has steadily risen since the 1980s, when the process of financialization began in earnest (see Figure 2.4).

Figure 2.4 shows the number of patents registered with the US Patent and Trademark Office (USPTO) for 1963–2020, grouping the results individually into registrations by Americans and by foreigners. Looking at total registrations, the number decreased from 68,405 in 1966 to 48,854 in 1979. However, since the 1980s, the number of patent registrations has continuously risen, reaching 65,771 in 1981, 147,517 in 1998, 219,614 in 2010, and 388,861 in 2020. Thus, the number soared 5.7 times during the analysis period. Breaking down the results by nationality, the number of patents registered by Americans and by foreigners increased at a similar overall rate. However, since the 2008 financial crisis, the number of registrations by foreigners has surpassed registration by Americans.

Patent registrations—both in terms of total numbers and in terms of the nationality-grouped numbers—have been rising steadily numerically since the 1980s, when financialization first began to take off. How can this phenomenon be explained? To answer this question, consider first that some recent studies indicate that financialization may lead to a higher propensity to patent. An increase in patent propensity

$\left(\dfrac{\text{number of patent registrations}}{\text{number of inventions}} \right)$ means that innovators, including

companies, are patenting more inventions than they did previously. The number of patent registrations is determined by the following equation that considers the impact of propensity to patent and the number of inventions:

$$\begin{aligned}
\text{number of patent registrations} \\
= \left(\frac{\text{number of patent registrations}}{\text{number of inventions}} \right) \\
\times \text{number of inventions} \\
= \text{patent propensity} \times \text{number of inventions}
\end{aligned}$$

This equation shows that the number of patent registrations increases as patent propensity rises. This can hold true even if the number of inventions does not change. In the past, because of the strictness of patent examinations, excessive costs of maintaining patents, lengthy patent examination schedules, and a general lack of confidence in the usefulness of patent protections, inventors often preferred to protect their inventions by keeping them secret, rather than by registering them.

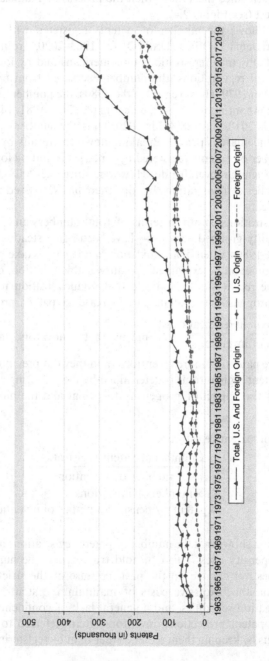

Figure 2.4 Total number of patent registrations in the United States (grouped by nationality).

Source: USPTO database.

As a result, patent propensity was relatively low. However, since the 1980s, the patent propensity of firms has risen thanks to the increasing strategic importance of patents, such as through their role, along with licenses, in blocking market entry by competitors, and in technology standardization and marketing (Gilbert and Newbery, 1982).

In addition, the number of patents that a start-up venture holds is used in IPO evaluations and credit ratings, and this has also encouraged higher patent propensity (Hochberg, Serrano, and Ziedonis, 2018). Also, as financialization has deepened, more and more firms are funding R&D efforts through the stock market and the number of patents held by firms has become an important firm valuation factor for attracting funding. As a result, the patent propensity of companies has risen (Hall, Jaffe, and Trajtenberg, 2005; Greenhalgh and Rogers, 2006; Deng, Lev, and Narin, 1999).

If further financialization leads to higher company patent propensity, it is possible that the trajectory of rising patent registrations may not seem to align with the above conclusion that financialization drives lower investment in innovation. However, from a qualitative standpoint, patent quality may fall due to short-termism of innovation. Thus, the effects of financialization on the quantitative and qualitative aspects of innovation may differ, with the two aspects varying independently of each other.

Measurement indicators related to corporate finance

Investigation into the micro and macro effects of financialization is preconditioned on availability of appropriate indicators of financialization. Household-level financialization measured as the ratio of household financial assets to total assets serves as the basis for the Aglietta (2000) analysis into household financialization and consumption. At the industry level, some studies employ the proportion of the finance, insurance, and real estate (FIRE) sector in overall employment and value-added production when estimating micro and macro changes caused by the rise of the FIRE sector (Kus, 2012; Darcillon, 2015).

The impact of financialization on macro variables such as consumption, investment, and income distribution can be measured using the ratio of interest and dividend income to GDP to represent financialization of the economic growth regime—meaning, financial sector growth at the macroeconomic level (Stockhammer, 2004). International investment position (IIP) is also an index for analyzing the effects of financialization in international transactions (Eatwell and Taylor, 2002; Seo et al., 2015).

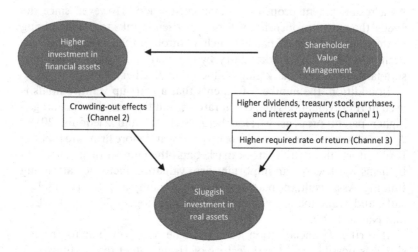

Figure 2.5 Channels through which financialization impacts real investment.

Studies of financialization in the corporate sector by Stockhammer (2004), Crotty (2005), Duménil and Lévy (2000), Aglietta and Breton (2001), and Orhangazi (2008) delve into the emergence of management practices emphasizing shareholder value. Such studies conclude that the emphasis on shareholder value hampers investment and employment activities. Figure 2.5 provides a schematic view of the effects of financialization on real investment. Though each of these study measures financialization with different variables, each pursue the same research objectives.

The Channel 1 impact of financialization (shown in Figure 2.5) assumes that higher corporate interest payments and dividends encroach on internal monetary reserves, resulting in lower real investment. To measure these effects, some studies instrumentalize financialization using dividend propensity and the ratio of total dividends and treasury stock purchases to net income (Orhangazi, 2008; Davis, 2018; Seo et al., 2012). In other studies, the extent of corporate financial outlays to the financial markets are represented by dividends, treasury stock purchases, and interest payments divided by total assets (Orhangazi, 2008; Seo et al., 2012).

The Channel 2 impact looks at the emergence of managerial myopia, in which the emphasis on maximizing shareholder value has shifted the priorities of managers away from growth-oriented strategies toward short-term profits. As a result, companies have increased their spending on financial assets, crowding out real investments. To better understand this channel, studies use the ratio of corporate financial assets to total assets (Seo et al., 2012) or profits from financial assets investment to total assets (Orhangazi, 2008; Seo et al., 2012).

Lastly, corporate performance is not merely evaluated based on whether a company has generated positive net income, but whether it has met the minimum rate of return required by the market. Channel 3 illustrates how investment plans may be scrapped or scaled back if they are not expected to achieve a minimum required rate of return, even if such investment might still have generated a positive net income. Aglietta and Rebérioux (2005) look at the Channel 3 process through the lens of EVA.

Conclusion and summary

The literature demonstrates that the influence of financial institutions, financial markets, and financiers on society has grown over the past 30 years. The results of this study can be broadly summarized as follows.

First, the process of financialization encompasses a variety of economic phenomena associated with the growing impact of finance: emergence of shareholder value management; increased importance of capital markets in raising capital; greater influence of rentiers, including financiers, in politics and the economy; explosive growth in domestic and international financial transactions; and changes in the growth regime. Quantitative indicators used to measure financialization include the following: share of financial assets in household assets, share of financial assets held by companies, dividend payout ratio, share of value-added production and employment in the financial industry, share of interest and dividend income in GDP, and magnitude of international financial transactions. Studies using these variables confirm that financialization has brought about structural changes to households, businesses, industries, national economies, and the global economy.

Second, empirical studies of financialization in OECD and developing countries demonstrate that the growing influence of financial markets and financial systems on corporate management is closely linked to the decline in corporate investment in facilities and equipment and to sluggish employment.

Third, recent empirical studies also demonstrate that financialization is closely related to global financial crises and widening income inequality.

Notes

1 Household financialization refers to the growing tendency for households to base consumption and savings decisions on financial income rather than earned income. The process toward great household financialization started with financial deregulation and demographic changes. As institutional investors managed more and more household savings collectively, it became increasingly important for those investors to maximize financial returns through the rationalization of asset portfolios. Likewise, households themselves reduced holdings of low-return bank deposits and increased the proportion of securities with higher expected returns. In addition, investment goals have gradually focused on the management of financial assets, rather than on securing short-term liquidity. Income inequality has been rising in terms of earned income; household financialization has further added property income inequity to this trend. As financial regulations eased and investors came to enjoy greater financial autonomy, households—not only as investors but also as debtors—saw their net worth become ever more enmeshed in the financial markets, both quantitatively and qualitatively. Household prosperity has become ever more closely correlated with trends in the financial markets through a myriad of financial instruments: insurance (health, fire, automobile, unemployment, etc.), retirement pensions, bank savings, and loans (student, home equity, consumer, etc.).

2 Industrial financialization refers to the relative strengthening of the financial sector compared to the non-financial sector through the financial sector's role in financing and evaluating credit to companies. In the late 1970s, as the rate of return on financial assets began to rise above the rate of return on real assets thanks to higher interest rates and greater financial liberalization, capital flowed from the non-financial sector to the financial sector. Financial markets have developed mechanisms for non-financial companies to act in accordance with financial norms (public evaluation of companies by financial institutions, development of new financial techniques and new financial products, etc.). This process of industrial financialization has transferred wealth from the non-financial sector to the financial sector. As a result, the relative economic weight of the financial and insurance service sectors has soared in terms of employment and value creation.

3 Growth regime financialization primarily means that, as finance rises to the top of the institutional hierarchy, emerging financial norms restrict the decisions of other non-financial institutions, leading to institutional transformations that bring about greater complementarity between the non-financial and financial sectors. Secondarily, growth regime financialization may also refer to the phenomenon in which the economic and political dominance of the rentier class becomes entrenched. As a result, efforts to promote the wage–labor relationship—which was the dominant inter-institutional relationship of the growth regime during the Fordism period—are subordinated to pressures to increase investment returns, thus resulting in the adoption of flexible labor strategies. Competition has also shifted from product markets

to financial markets. In terms of income distribution, the proportion of interest and dividend income is growing. With household consumption being the driving force for growth, rising household debt to fund higher consumption promotes systemic instability. Investment remains sluggish due to efforts to maximize shareholder value, and financial market deregulation leads to repeated financial crises. Régulation theory defines this growth system as a "finance-led accumulation regime."

4 International transaction financialization refers to the process in which financial norms are globalized, this process having accelerated in the 1990s with globalization, deregulation, and greater economic openness. The Washington Consensus for the globalization of finance became the basis of policy, and the erosion of time and space constraints opened the global financial markets to new investment portfolio possibilities. International transaction financialization brought capital from emerging Asian countries and oil-exporting nations to the United States. These capital inflows resulted in a huge US trade deficit, while also allowing the US to maintain investment at constant levels despite the low domestic savings rate. According to McKinsey estimates, global financial assets amounted to USD 12 trillion, or 120% of global GDP, in the 1980s. By 2010, this figure was USD 219 trillion, or 316% of global GDP (TNI, 2015). In 2012, the daily international trade volume of goods and services was USD 58.9 billion, while daily trading volume in international foreign exchange markets hit USD 5.3 trillion in 2013. In other words, the amount of financial trading was approximately 90 times that of goods and services trading.

References

Aglietta, M. (2000), "Shareholder value and corporate governance: Some tricky questions," *Economy and Society*, Vol. 29, No. 1, pp. 146–159.

Aglietta, M. and R. Breton (2001), "Financial systems, corporate control and capital accumulation", *Economy and Society*, Vol. 30, No. 4, pp. 433–466.

Aglietta, M. and A. Rebérioux (2005), *Corporate governance adrift: A critique of shareholder value*, Cheltenham: Edward Elgar.

Berle, A. A. and G. C. Means (1932), *The modern corporation and private property*, New York: Commerce Clearing House.

Boyer, R. (2000), "Is a finance-led growth regime a viable alternative to Fordism? A preliminary analysis," *Economy and Society*, Vol. 29, No. 1, pp. 111–145.

Boyer, R. (2013), "The present crisis. A trump for a renewed political economy," *Review of Political Economy*, Vol. 25, No. 1, pp. 1–38.

Crotty, J. (2005), "The neoliberal paradox: The impact of destructive product market competition and 'modern' financial markets on nonfinancial corporation performance in the neoliberal era," in Epstein, A. G. (ed.), *Financialization and the world economy*, Northampton, MA: Edward Elgar.

Darcillon, T. (2015), "How does finance affect labor market institutions? An empirical analysis in 16 OECD countries," *Socio-Economic Review*, Vol. 13, No. 3, pp. 477–504.

42 *Financialization and corporate innovation strategy*

Davis, L. E. (2018), "Financialization and the non-financial corporation: An investigation of firm-level investment behavior in the United States," *Metroeconomica*, Vol. 69, No. 1, pp. 270–307.

Demir, F. (2009), "Financial liberalization, private investment and portfolio choice: Financialization of real sectors in emerging markets," *Journal of Development Economics*, Vol. 88, No. 2, pp. 314–324.

Deng, Z., B. Lev, and F. Narin (1999), "Science and technology as predictors of stock performance," *Financial Analysts Journal*, Vol. 55, No. 3, pp. 20–32.

Duménil, G. and D. Lévy (2000), *Crise et sortie de crise: Ordre et désordres néolibéraux*, Paris: PUF.

Duménil, G. and D. Lévy (2004), *Capital resurgent: Roots of the neoliberal revolution*, Cambridge, MA: Harvard University Press.

Eatwell, J. and L. Taylor (2002), "Introduction," in Eatwell, J. and L. Taylor (ed.), *International capital markets: Systems in transition*, New York: Oxford University Press.

Edmans, A., V. W. Fang, and K. A. Lewellen (2017), "Equity vesting and investment", *The Review of Financial Studies*, Vol. 30, No. 7, pp. 2229–2271.

Epstein, G. A. and A. Jayadev (2005), "The rise of rentier incomes in OECD countries: Financialization, central bank policy and labor solidarity," in Epstein, G. A. (ed.), *Financialization and the world economy*, Northampton, MA: Edward Elgar.

Froud, J., C. Haslam, S. Johal, and K. Williams (2000), "Shareholder value and financialization: Consultancy promises, management moves," *Economy and Society*, Vol. 29, No. 1, pp. 80–110.

Gilbert, R. J. and D. Newbery (1982), "Preemptive patenting and the persistence of monopoly," *American Economic Review*, Vol. 72, No. 3, pp. 514–526.

Greenhalgh, C. and M. Rogers (2006), "The value of innovation: The interaction of competition, R&D and IP," *Research Policy*, Vol. 35, No. 4, pp. 562–580.

Hall, B. H., A. Jaffe, and M. Trajtenberg (2005), "Market value and patent citations," *RAND Journal of Economics*, Vol. 36, No. 1, pp. 16–38.

Hein, E (2014), *Distribution and growth after Keynes*, Cheltenham: Edward Elgar.

Hochberg, Y. V., C. J. Serrano, and R. H. Ziedonis (2018), "Patent collateral, investor commitment, and the market for venture lending," *Journal of Financial Economics*, Vol. 130, No. 1, pp. 74–94.

Jensen, M. C. and W. H. Meckling (1976), "Theory of the firm: Managerial behavior, agency costs and ownership structure," *Journal of Financial Economics*, Vol. 3, No. 4, pp. 305–360.

Jibril, H., A. Kaltenbrunner, and E. Kesidou (2018), "Financialization and innovation in emerging economies: Evidence from Brazil," *Leeds University Business School Working Paper*, No. 18-09.

Konings, J. and H. Vandenbussche (1995), "The effect of foreign competition on UK employment and wages: Evidence from firm-level panel data," *Review of World Economy*, Vol. 131, pp. 655–672.

Krippner, G. R. (2005), "The financialization of the American economy," *Socio-Economic Review*, Vol. 3, No. 2, pp. 173–208.

Kus, B. (2012), "Financialization and income inequality in OECD nations:1995–2007," *The Economic and Social Review*, Vol. 43, No. 4, pp. 477–495.

Lazonick, W. and M. O'Sullivan (2000), "Maximization shareholder value: A new ideology for corporate governance," *Economy and Society*, Vol. 29, No. 1, pp. 13–35.

Lee, Y. S., H. S. Kim, and H. J. Seo (2020), "Financialization and innovation short-termism in OECD countries," *Review of Radical Political Economics*, Vol. 52, No. 2, pp. 259–286.

Lin, K. H. (2016), "The rise of finance and firm employment dynamics," *Organization Science*, Vol. 27, No. 4, pp. 972–988.

OECD (1998), "Shareholder value and market in corporate control in OECD countries," *Financial Market Trends*, Vol. 1998, No. 1, pp. 15–38.

Onaran, Ö., E. Stockhammer, and G. Lucas (2011), "Financialisation, income distribution and aggregate demand in the USA," *Cambridge Journal of Economics*, Vol. 35, No. 4, pp. 637–661.

Orhangazi, Ö. (2008), "Financialization and capital accumulation in the nonfinancial corporate sector: A theoretical and empirical investigation of the US economy, 1973-2004," *Cambridge Journal of Economics*, Vol. 32, No. 6, pp. 863–886.

Phillips, K. (2002), *Wealth and democracy: A political history of the American rich*, New York: Broadway Books.

Phillips, K (1994), *Arrogant capital: Washington, Wall Street, and the frustration of American politics*, New York: Little, Brown and Company.

Philips, K. (1993), *Boiling point*, New York: Random House.

Rodrik, D. (1997), *Has globalization gone too far?* Washington: Institute for international economics.

Seo H. J., H. S. Kim, and Y. S. Lee (2015), "Globalization and labor demand elasticities: Empirical evidence from nine OECD countries," *Korean Economic Review*, Vol. 31, No. 2, pp. 413–439.

Seo, H. J., H. S. Kim, and J. I. Kim (2016), "Does shareholder value orientation or financial market liberalization slow down Korean real investment?" *Review of Radical Political Economics*, Vol. 48, No. 4, pp. 633–660.

Seo, H. J., H. S. Kim, and Y. C. Kim (2012), "Financialization and the slowdown in Korean firms' R&D investment," *Asian Economic Papers*, Vol. 11, No. 3, pp. 35–49.

Sjöberg, O. (2009), "Corporate governance and earnings inequality in the OECD countries 1979–2000," *European Sociological Review*, Vol. 25, No. 5, pp. 519–533.

Skott, P. and S. Ryoo (2008), "Macroeconomic implications of financialization," *Cambridge Journal of Economics*, Vol. 32, No. 6, pp. 827–862.

Stockhammer, E. (2004), "Financialisation and the slowdown of accumulation," *Cambridge Journal of Economics*, Vol. 28, No. 5, pp. 719–741.

Stockhammer, E. (2005), "Shareholder value orientation and the investment-profit puzzle," *Journal of Post Keynesian Economics*, Vol. 28, No. 2, pp. 193–215.

Stockhammer, E. (2009), "Determinants of functional income distribution in OECD countries," *IMK Studies*, 05–2209.

Stout, L. (2012), *The shareholder value myth*, San Francisco: Berrett-Koehler Publishers.

TNI (2015), Financialization, Amsterdam: Transnational Institute.

Tridico, P. (2012), "Financial crisis and global imbalances: Its labor market origins and the aftermath," *Cambridge Journal of Economics*, Vol. 36, No. 1, pp. 17–42.

Wallerstein, M. (1999), "Wage-setting institutions and pay inequality in advanced industrialized societies," *American Journal of Political Science*, Vol. 43, No. 3, pp. 649–680.

Williams, K. (2000), "From shareholder value to present-day capitalism," *Economy and Society*, Vol. 29, No. 1, pp. 1–12.

Database

OECD database (https://data.oecd.org/, retrieved on October 10, 2021).

USPTO (www.uspto.gov/learning-and-resources/statistics, retrieved on October 15, 2021)

3 Innovative capacity and financialization of Korean firms

It is well known that the Republic of Korea (ROK) achieved rapid economic growth through strong government support for private enterprises. The main policy tools are the five-year economic plans (1962–1996) with strong leadership of the Economic Planning Board (EPB) with designated financial policies and huge investment on R&D-related institutions and researches. This chapter conducts a comparative study to compare Korea's innovative capacity. The rankings of the patent grants of the Korean companies are also compared. Finally, using the firm-level micro data, the innovative capacity and the degree of financialization are discussed.

General competitiveness

One of the popular of innovative capacity indicator is the World Competitiveness Yearbook (WCY) that is released by the IMD annually (IMD, 2021). First published in 1989, WCY ranks the countries by analyzing their competencies to achieve long-term creative capacity and value creation. WCY determines three rankings, World Competitiveness ranking, World Digital Competitiveness ranking, and World Talent ranking, in which the 2021 edition covers 64 countries with 334, 51, and 32 criteria, respectively. For the general World Competitiveness ranking, the main categories are economic performance, government efficiency, business efficiency, and infrastructure.

The final category, infrastructure, consists of basic infrastructure, technological infrastructure, scientific infrastructure, health and environment, and education. Thus, scientific infrastructure reflects the innovative capacity. In addition, the three main categories of the World Digital Competitiveness ranking are knowledge, technology, and future readiness, while the World Talent ranking is assessed based on investment and development, appeal, and readiness factors.

DOI: 10.4324/9781003240822-3

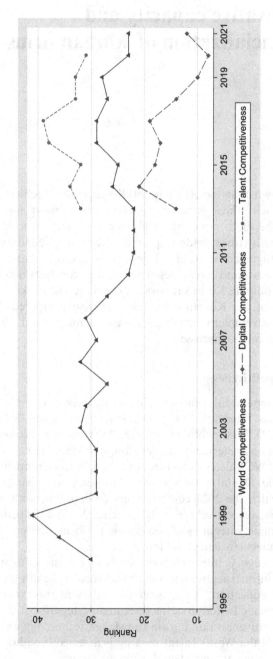

Figure 3.1 Trend of ROK IMD competitiveness ranking.
Source: IMD World Competitiveness Online (accessed on Oct 27, 2021).

Figure 3.1 shows the trends of the World Competitiveness ranking, ranking of digital competitiveness, and talent competitiveness of ROK. In 1995, among 64 countries, ROK was ranked at 30th in the overall competitiveness and then ranked at 29 and 23 in 2017 and 2021, respectively. By categories, in 2021, ROK ranked 18th in economic performance, 34th in government efficiency, 27th in business efficiency, and 17th in infrastructure. Specifically, by criteria, ROK showed weak performance in business legislation (49), prices (51), and labor market (37) situations. However, ROK particularly ranked high in scientific infrastructure (2), domestic economy (5), employment (5), and technological infrastructure (17) situations.

As figure shows, ROK ranked 12th in digital competitiveness in 2021, with the highest ranking of 8th in 2020, reflecting strong innovative competitiveness. On the other hand, the talent competitiveness ranking of ROK was 31st in 2020, demonstrating a weak performance compared to the other two competitiveness rankings throughout the sample period. This indicates the ability of ROK with regards motivating, developing, and retaining its talent needs further progress.

Various researcher and R&D expenditure indicators

The following tables compare various researcher and R&D expenditure indicators. Table 3.1 summarizes the total R&D expenditure and per capita R&D expenditure by country in 2019. In terms of total R&D

Table 3.1 R&D expenditure indicators by country (2019)

Total R&D expenditure (million USD)			Per capita R&D expenditure (USD)		
Rank	Country	Amount	Rank	Country	Amount
1	USA	657,459	1	Israel	2,152
2	China	320,532	2	USA	2,001
3	Japan	164,709	3	Sweden	1,760
4	Germany	123,171	4	Denmark	1,753
5	ROK	76,712	5	Norway	1,633
6	France	59,932	6	Iceland	1,902
7	UK	49,707	7	Austria	1,569
8	Italy	29,397	8	Germany	1,482
9	Canada	27,719	9	ROK	1,478
10	Netherland	19,882	10	Belgium	1,472

Source: NTIS

expenditure, the United States ranked 1st with 657,459 million USD, followed by China (320,532 million USD), Japan (164,709 million USD), and Germany (123,171 million USD). ROK was ranked 5th with 76,712 million USD. Thus, ROK has a higher R&D expenditure than other developed countries (France, the UK, Italy, etc.).

However, per capita R&D expenditure demonstrates different ranking of the countries. This ranking shows the R&D potential. Israel was ranked 1st with 2,152 USD, and the United States (2,001 USD), Sweden (1,760 USD), Denmark (1,753 USD), and Norway (1,633) followed. The ranking of ROK falls to 9th in terms of per capita R&D expenditure with 1,478 USD. However, the ranking of per capita R&D (9th) is higher than that of per capita income (about 40th); this ranking is still higher than other developed countries. Moreover, the United States had similar rankings for both R&D expenditure indicators.

Table 3.2 shows the R&D expenditure by research institutions in 2019. The research institutions consist of government, university, enterprises, and non-profit institutions. In most of the countries, most research is conducted by enterprises.

Furthermore, the United States, which is regarded as the most market-oriented country, shows the share of research funded by the government (9.9%) is higher than that of Japan (7.8%) but almost the same as ROK (10.0%). Among the top 10 countries for R&D expenditure, China (15.5%) has the highest share of government, while Netherland (5.7%) demonstrates the lowest share of research funded by the government.

In addition, 41.5% of Canada's R&D expenditure is by universities, more than five times greater than that of ROK (8.2%) and China (8.1%).

Table 3.2 R&D expenditure by research institutions (2019)

Country	Government	University	Enterprises	Non-profit Institutions	Total
USA	64,961(9.9)	78,717(12.0)	485,826(73.9)	27,954(4.3)	657,458
China	49,580(15.5)	26,006(8.1)	244,946(76.4)	-	320,532
Japan	12,866(7.8)	19,258(11.7)	130,374(79.2)	2,211(1.3)	164,709
Germany	16,817(13.7)	21,463(17.4)	84,890(68.9)	-	123,171
ROK	7,636(10.0)	6,326(8.2)	61,360(80.0)	1,090(1.4)	76,712
France	7,417(12.4)	12,034(20.1)	39,428(65.8)	1,054(1.8)	59,932
UK	3,274(6.6)	11,472(23.1)	33,121(66.6)	1,147(2.3)	49,707
Italy	3,702(12.6)	6,602(22.5)	18,571(63.2)	522(1.8)	29,397
Canada	2,076(7.5)	11,501(41.5)	14,033(50.6)	109(0.4)	27,719
Netherland	1,135(5.7)	5,485(27.6)	13,261(66.7)	0	19,881

Note: Unit: million USD, %

Source: NTIS.

In the UK and Italy, the share of R&D conducted by universities is 23.1% and 22.5%, respectively. Thus it can be inferred that in European countries a greater proportion of R&D is conducted by universities. In the United States and Japan universities conducted less R&D than that of European countries.

The share of R&D expenditure conducted by the enterprises is relatively higher than those by other institutions. The highest share of enterprises is in ROK. In total, 80.0% of research is conducted by enterprises, which is the highest share in the top 10 countries in R&D expenditure. Next was the shares of Japan and China, which were 79.2% and 76.4%, respectively. Interestingly, the East Asian countries that are considered to have adopted a government-led economic development strategy show a higher share of research by enterprises, by universities.

Table 3.3 shows R&D expenditure by funding source. Due to the difference in data source and classification, the values of total R&D expenditure in the last column of this table are not exactly the same as those in other tables. For the United States, the total R&D expenditure in Table 3.1 was 657,459 million USD while that in Table 3.3 was 656,559 million USD.

As Table 3.3 shows, most of the research funding is from private sectors, where China shows the highest share of private sectors with 99.9% (244,344 million USD). Japan (78.9% with 129,976 million USD) and ROK (77.0% with 58,799 million USD) follow. On the other hand, Russia shows the lowest private sector share with 30.2%

Table 3.3 R&D expenditure by funding sources (2019)

Country	Private	Foreign	Public	Total
USA	416,256(63.4)	48,032(7.3)	192,271(29.3)	656,559(100)
China	244,344(99.9)	346(0.1)	-	244,690(100)
Japan	129,976(78.9)	963(0.6)	33,770(20.6)	164,709(100)
Germany	79,392(64.5)	9,087(7.4)	34,691(52.5)	123,170(100)
ROK	58,799(77.0)	1,227(1.6)	16,386(21.4)	76,412(100)
France	33,958(56.7)	4,817(8.0)	21,159(35.3)	59,934(100)
UK	27,103(54.8)	6,762(13.7)	15,594(31.5)	49,459(100)
Canada	11,550(41.7)	2,502(9.0)	13,667(49.3)	27,719(100)
Russia	5,296(30.2)	420(2.4)	11,813(67.4)	17,529(100)
Netherland	11,451(57.6)	2,065(10.4)	6,365(32.0)	19,881(100)

Note: UK is for 2018.

Unit: million USD, %

Source: NTIS.

(5,296 million USD). Thus Russia demonstrates the highest share of public sources (67.4%). Other countries have more than 50% of R&D funded privately. This trend reflects a high share of R&D conducted by enterprises as shown in Table 3.2. Interestingly, Germany also has a relatively higher share of public funds for R&D with only 64.5% of private funds, even though this share was lower than that of Russia (67.4%). For foreign funding sources, the UK has the highest share of 13.7% (6,762 million USD). Among the top 10 countries, the United States receives the most foreign funds of 48,032 million USD, while the share of R&D expenditure funded by foreign sources is the highest in the UK with 13.7%.

For ROK, the shares of private funds and public funds are 77.0% (58,799 million USD) and 21.4% (16,386 million USD), respectively. It can be compared with the research institutions. The 61,360 million USD (80.0%) of R&D expenditure was undertaken by enterprises. However, the funding by private institutions was 58,799 million USD (77.0%). It can be inferred that the R&D research of the private sectors was partly financed by public funding.

Table 3.4 summarizes the amount of R&D expenditure by development stage in 2019. Research aims to acquire new scientific knowledge that underlies observables, without aiming specific application or use. Using knowledge as a result of basic research, applied research aims to acquire new scientific knowledge with a practical purpose and global

Table 3.4 R&D expenditure by development stage

Country	Basic research	Applied research	Development research	Others	Total
USA	107,838(16.4)	124,849(19.0)	423,352(64.4)	1,420(0.2)	657,639
China	19,333(6.0)	36,166(11.3)	265,034(82.7)	–	320,533
Japan	20,583(12.5)	30,579(18.6)	106,722(64.8)	6,826(4.1)	164,710
France	13,878(22.7)	25,263(41.3)	22,078(36.1)	–	61,219
ROK	11,209(15.7)	17,197(24.1)	43,006(60.2)	–	71,412
UK	9,041(18.3)	20,802(42.1)	19,619(39.7)		49,462
Italy	6,465(21.7)	12,081(40.6)	11,198(37.6)	–	29,744
Israel	1,947(10.0)	1,975(10.1)	15,552(79.9)	–	19,474
Netherland	4,308(26.1)	7,262(43.9)	4,967(30.0)	–	16,537
Spain	3,715(21.0)	7,253(41.1)	6,682(37.9)	–	17,650
Denmark	1,859(18.5)	3,124(31.1)	5,064(50.4)	–	10,047

Note: France, the UK, Italy, Netherland, and Denmark are for 2018.
Unit: million USD, %
Source: NTIS; OECD database.

original research. Using knowledge from basic and applied research, development research indicates the systematic activities for substantially improving the installation of a service, the production of new materials, products and devices, new processes, and systems that were already installed, or produced (NTIS).

Most countries concentrate their R&D expenditure on development research except the European countries.

In addition, European countries tend to focus more on the applied research area than other stages. For example, the proportion of R&D expenditure of France, UK, Italy, Netherland, and Spain is highest in the applied research stage with 41.3%, 42.1%, 40.6%, 43.9%, and 41.1%, respectively. Moreover, out of the top 10 countries, Netherland has the highest share in the stage of basic research (26.1%), while China demonstrates the highest share in development research (82.7% with 265,304 million USD). Israel also spends relatively more on development research (79.9% with 15,552 million USD) than other countries.

The United States as the country with the highest amount spent on R&D shows a share of 16.4% in basic research, 19.0% in applied research, and 64.4% in development research. The countries that have more than 40% of R&D expenditure in applied research stage are France, the UK, Italy, and Israel. Moreover, ROK invests a R&D expenditure of 15.7% in basic research, 24.1% in applied research, and 60.2% in development research. Therefore, it can be inferred that ROK tends to spend more on the development stage even though the share (60.2%) was lower than those of China (82.7%), Israel (79.9%), Japan (64.8%), and the United States (64.4%).

Table 3.5 shows two indicators of R&D expenditure intensity on basic research measured by the share to GDP in 2019 and the amount of R&D expenditure on high-tech industries in 2018.

While ROK ranked 5th highest in the volume of R&D expenditure on basic research as shown in Table 3.4 and even in the total amount of R&D expenditure as shown in Table 3.1, ROK demonstrates the highest R&D expenditure intensity on basic research with 0.68% of GDP in 2019. The Netherlands and Austria both follow with 0.55% of GDP. The United States with the highest amount of R&D expenditure ranked 6th highest with 0.50. China was the 2nd highest in R&D expenditure but was not ranked in the top 10 countries for R&D intensity.

For the R&D expenditure on the high-tech industry, the United States spends the highest amount with 182,580 million USD in 2018. Japan and ROK follow with 38,548 and 34,084 million USD, respectively. Interestingly, only three countries (ROK, Czech Republic, and the United States) ranked as top 10 countries in both the R&D expenditure

Table 3.5 R&D expenditure intensity and expenditure on high-tech industry

R&D expenditure on basic research to GDP (2019)			R&D expenditure on high-tech industry (2018) million USD		
Rank	Country	Share(%)	Rank	Country	Amount
1	ROK	0.68	1	USA	182,580
2	Netherlands	0.55	2	Japan	38,548
3	Austria	0.55	3	ROK	34,084
4	Denmark	0.53	4	Germany	17,967
5	Czech Republic	0.51	5	UK	17,967
6	USA	0.50	6	Italy	3,396
7	Israel	0.49	7	Spain	1,671
8	Luxembourg	0.44	8	Poland	408
9	Iceland	0.43	9	Norway	314
10	Greece	0.41	10	Czech Republic	2456

Note: France, the UK, Italy, Netherland, and Denmark are for 2018.
Unit: million USD, %
Source: NTIS; OECD database.

intensity on basic research and the R&D expenditure on high-tech industry.

Table 3.6 shows two indicators of the share of Ph.D. and master's degrees out of total engineering researchers in 2018. France has the highest share of Ph.D. degrees with 48.8%. Chile and Czech Republic follow with 48.3% and 47.7%, respectively. ROK has 37.6% of Ph.D. degrees out of the total engineering researchers.

However, the ranking of the share of engineers to total master's degrees shows different rankings. The top country is Japan with 42.2%, followed by Portugal and Germany with 32.4% and 30.8%, respectively. ROK ranked similarly in both indicators, by ranking 24th in the former indicator and ranking 21st in the latter indicator. Therefore, it can be inferred that ROK tends to have a relatively low share of engineers to total Ph.D. and master's degrees. The results can contrast greatly with the high rankings of various R&D expenditure indicators discussed above such as high R&D expenditure intensity and/or amount of R&D expenditure.

Performance in articles and patents

With R&D expenditure, each economic unit produces outcomes, ranging from the number of article publication to application and registration of patents. Here, two different R&D performances are compared.

Table 3.6 Share of engineering researchers by degree

Share of engineers to total Ph.D. degrees (2018)			Share of engineers to total master's degrees (2018)		
Rank	Country	Share (%)	Rank	Country	Amount
1	France	48.8	1	Japan	42.2
2	Chile	48.3	2	Portugal	32.4
3	Czech Republic	47.7	3	Germany	30.8
4	Luxembourg	47.4	4	Russia	28.5
5	Italy	47.4	5	Sweden	28.1
6	Canada	47.4	6	Brazil	26.4
7	Switzerland	46.7	7	Italy	24.5
8	Estonia	46.3	8	Estonia	24.1
9	Israel	45.7	9	New Zealand	23.8
10	Latvia	45.5	10	Norway	23.7
24	ROK	37.6	21	ROK	20.0

Note: The total number of countries is 40.
Source: NTIS; OECD database.

Table 3.7 Number of articles and citations in science and technologies

Number of articles in science and technology (2018)			Number of citations per article by five-year period (2015–2019)		
Rank	Country	Number	Rank	Country	Number
1	China	491,960	1	Iceland	13.3
2	USA	484,819	2	Estonia	12.4
3	UK	154,906	3	Singapore	11.9
4	Germany	130,817	4	Luxembourg	11.6
5	Japan	89,896	5	Switzerland	10.8
6	Canada	86,241	6	Denmark	10.7
7	Italy	85,162	7	Netherlands	9.9
8	France	84,811	8	Belgium	9.8
9	Australia	84,456	9	Sweden	9.6
10	Spain	73,240	10	Ireland	9.5
11	ROK	69,618	34	ROK	6.9

Note: The total number of countries is 40.
Source: NTIS.

Table 3.7 lists the number of articles in science & technology (S&T) and the number of citations per article by 5 year period. For the number of articles in S&T, China is 1st, and USA and UK are 2nd and 3rd with 484,819 and 154,906, respectively, in 2018. This indicator reflects the quantity aspect of innovation capacity. However, the number of citations reflects the qualitative aspect of the innovation. Rankings of citation per article are different from the number of articles. Iceland ranked 1st in the number of citations per article by five-year period. Estonia and Singapore follow with 12.4 and 11.9, respectively. China and USA, which were the 1st and 2nd highest in the quantity indicator, are not in the top 10 countries in the quality indicator. Interestingly, the top 10 countries in the number of articles in S&T are different from the top countries in the number of citations per article by five-year period.

ROK ranked 11th highest in the number of articles published in the S&T journals in 2018. However, the ranking of quality of the articles published goes down to 34th for the 2015–2019 period. This indicator suggests that the policy to promote innovation capacity needs to focus more on the quality of the article publication relative to their quantity.

Table 3.8 ranks the countries by the number of triadic patents and the number of patents applied to the Patent Cooperation Treaty (PCT) in 2019. The triadic patents are the number of patents applied to the European Patent Office (EPO), the Japan Patent Office (JPO), and the United States Patent and Trademark Office (USPTO). Therefore, the number of triadic patents will reflect the higher quality of patents than the patents that are separately registered in each of the patent office. Japan and the United States ranked 1st and 2nd, respectively, in the number of triadic patents per 1 million population, and ROK was ranked 5th.

Table 3.8 Number of triadic patents and patents applied to PCT

Triadic patents per 1 million population (2019)			Number of patents applied to PCT (2020)		
Rank	*Country*	*Number*	*Rank*	*Country*	*Number*
1	Japan	17,702.40	1	China	68,751
2	USA	12,881.40	2	USA	58,836
3	Germany	4,620.70	3	Japan	50,543
4	China	5,596.60	4	ROK	20,056
5	ROK	2,558.00	5	Germany	18,540
6	France	1,856.60	6	France	7,765
7	UK	1,690.10	7	UK	5,903
8	Switzerland	1,225.30	8	Switzerland	4,901
9	Netherlands	957.3	9	Sweden	4,351
10	Italy	947.4	10	Netherlands	4,011

Source: NTIS

Table 3.9 Number of patents registered to USPTO and EPO

Patents registered in USPTO (2019)			Patents registered in EPO (2019)		
Rank	Country	number	Rank	Country	Number
1	USA	167,115	1	USA	34,616
2	Japan	53,542	2	Japan	22,426
3	ROK	21,684	3	Germany	21,189
4	China	19,209	4	France	8,796
5	Germany	18,293	5	ROK	7,251
6	UK	7,791	6	China	6,228
7	Canada	7,595	7	Switzerland	4,793
8	France	7,233	8	Netherlands	4,326
9	India	5,378	9	UK	4,122
10	Israel	4,681	10	Sweden	3,854

Source: NTIS; WIPO, Statistics database

Second, the number of patents applied to the PCT in 2020 is shown. The PCT is the international treaty signed in 1978 to protect the inconvenience in the patent application process in foreign country. China, which ranked 4th for triadic patents per 1 million population, was 1st in the number of patents applied to the PCT. The United States and Japan follow as 2nd and 3rd, and ROK ranked 4th.

Table 3.9 shows the ranking of the patents registered to the USPTO and the EPO, respectively. The United States, Japan, ROK, China, Germany, UK, and France ranked in the top 10 countries in both patent offices in 2019. Specifically, the United States and Japan ranked the 1st and the 2nd in the number of patents registered in both the USPTO and the EPO. China with the 2nd highest in R&D expenditure ranked 4th in patents registered in the USPTO and 6th in the number of patents registered in the EPO.

ROK ranked 3rd in patent registration in the USPTO and 5th in patent registration in the EPO worldwide. It is noticeable that the rankings of the patent registration are similar to the R&D expenditure rankings. However, it should be noted that the ranking of the number of citations per article by 5 year period in Table 3.7 is much lower than rankings of R&D expenditures and other R&D performances such as registration of patents and the number of article publications.

Unlike the rankings by country above, Table 3.10 lists the patent performance of ROK enterprises to evaluate the innovation capacity. In addition to the top 10 ranking companies, the rankings of major Korean companies are added. For the 10-year period, there is a notable change

Table 3.10 Korea's most innovative companies

2020			2010		
Rank	Companies	Patents	Rank	Companies	Patents
1	International Business Machines Corporation	9,118	1	International Business Machines Corporation	5,866
2	Samsung Electronics Co., Ltd.	6,396	2	Samsung Electronics Co., Ltd.	4,518
3	Canon Kabushiki Kaisha	3,225	3	Microsoft Corporation	3,086
4	Microsoft Technology Licensing	2,909	4	Canon Kabushiki Kaisha	2,551
5	Intel Corporation	2,865	5	Panasonic Corporation	2,443
6	LG Electronics Inc.	2,830	6	Toshiba Corporation	2,212
7	Taiwan Semiconductor Manufacturing Co., Ltd.	2,817	7	Sony Corporation	2,130
8	Apple, Inc.	2,788	8	Intel Corporation	1,652
9	Huawei Technologies Co. Ltd.	2,760	9	LG Electronics Inc.	1,488
10	Qualcomm, Inc.	2,276	10	Hewlett-Packard Development Company, LP	1,480
14	Samsung Display	1,892	19	Hynix Semiconductor	973
20	Hyundai Motor	11874	34	LG Display	737
32	LG Display	989	60	Samsung SDI	438
35	LG Chem.	944	77	Samsung Mobile	335
38	SK Hynix	924	91	Samsung Electro-Mechanics	272

Source: USPTO.

in the rankings. Nevertheless, the International Business Machine Corporation ranked 1st in both 2010 and 2020 with 9,118 and 5,866 patent grants, respectively. In addition, Samsung Electronics, which is regarded as the top Korean company, was the 2nd highest in both 2010 and 2020 with 4,518 and 6,396 patent grants, respectively. Over the years, the rankings and number of patent grants of Korean companies tend to increase. For example, for the top 50 ranking companies in 2010, four ROK companies (Samsung Electronics, LG Electronics, Hynix Semiconductor, and LG Display) are included. However, in 2020, the number increased to seven companies (Samsung Electronics,

Table 3.11 Global exports market share of high-tech industries (2019)

Country	Pharmaceutical (%)	Computer/electronics/ optical (%)	Aerospace (%)
USA	8.84	7.29	30.14
Germany	14.08	4.98	11.81
China	2.67	26.19	1.59
France	5.57	1.32	15.53
UK	4.37	1.26	9.42
Switzerland	4.37	1.22	0.50
Singapore	1.35	4.78	4.95
Netherlands	4.59	2.70	1.29
Ireland	8.49	0.74	1.29
Italy	5.41	0.64	1.50
ROK	0.64	5.63	0.60

LG Electronics, Samsung Display, Hyundai Motor, LG Display, LG Chem., and SK Hynix INC.).

Table 3.11 lists the global exports market share of three high-tech industries (pharmaceutical, computer/electronics/optical, and aerospace) in 2019. Out of 11 countries, Germany has the highest exports market share in the pharmaceutical industry with 14.08%. The United States (8.84%) and Ireland (8.49%) follow. For the computer, electronics, and optical industry, China has the highest exports market share with 26.19%, followed by the United States (7.29%), ROK (5.63%), Germany (4.98%), and Singapore (4.78%). For the aerospace industry, the United States has 30.14% of the exports market. France (15.53%) and Germany (11.81%) follow.

ROK, which has the top-ranked amount and share of R&D expenditure and number of patent registrations, has a relatively low exports market share. The market share of the pharmaceutical industry was 0.64% and that of the aerospace industry was 0.60%. Only the market share of the computer, electronics, and optical industry was 5.63% next to China and the United States. Therefore, it suggests that ROK needs to invest more on the high-tech industry in addition to the computer, electronics, and optical industry.

Table 3.12 lists the countries by government or enterprises' R&D expenditure on the aerospace industry, space industry, and biotechnology industry.

For the aerospace industry, in 2018, the enterprises budget of the United States was 24,290 million USD. Other countries are much behind. The UK as the country ranked 2nd spent 2,099 million USD,

Table 3.12 R&D expenditure indicators on high-tech industries

Country	Aerospace industry budget of enterprises (2018)	Country	Government R&D budget for space industry (2019)	Country	Enterprise R&D expenditure on biotechnology (2017)
USA	24,290	USA	10,153	USA	51,637
UK	2,099	Japan	2,157	Switzerland	3,899
Germany	2,016	France	2,081	France	3,840
Italy	1,402	Germany	1,718	Belgium	3,461
Japan	744	Italy	1,256	ROK	1,718
Canada	722	Spain	395	Denmark	1,682
Spain	540	ROK	329	Germany	1,433
ROK	326	Belgium	256	Spain	1,060
Poland	62	UK	198	Italy	726
Czech Republic	48	Netherlands	146	Canada	564

Unit: Million USD.

which is about 10% of the expenditure of the United States. Germany and Italy follow with 2,016 and 1,402 million USD, respectively.

The United States ranked 1st in the government budget for the space industry in 2019 and the enterprises' R&D expenditure on bio-technology in 2017. For the government R&D budget for space industry, Japan and France as the 2nd and 3rd highest spent 2,157 and 2,081 million USD, respectively. For enterprises' R&D expenditure on biotechnology, Switzerland and France were ranked 2nd and 3rd with 3,899 and 3,840 million USD.

ROK also spent a large budget on these industries. It ranked 8th for the aerospace industry, 7th for the space industry, and 5th for the bio-technology industry.

Recent trends in innovation performance and financialization

The two top-level indicators of this study are innovation performance and degree of financialization.

Innovation performance is measured using (1) number of patents granted by the USPTO and (2) number of citations accumulated by those patents. The bulk dataset was taken from the USPTO website and cleaned by extracting patents for which ROK is the country of the rep-resentative assignee. The 277,281 patents registered for Korea received

540,860 accumulated citations between 1979 and 2020. Of these patents, the authors then used only those for which the assignee was registered as an organization. This brought the numbers down to 272,189 granted patents, with 537,657 accumulated citations. Patent citations are linked to the year in which the respective patent was granted.

There are four indicators of financialization in this study: (1) ratio of total payout to net profit (RTP), (2) ratio of dividend payout to net profit (RDP), (3) ratio of financial asset investment (RFA), and (4) ratio of profits of financial assets (RPFA). All financialization data was downloaded from the KISVALUE database. As of 2019, this data included 948 KOSPI (Korea Stock Price Index) companies, 1,510 KOSDAQ (Korea Securities Dealers Automated Quotation) companies, and 27,706 unlisted companies.

From the USTPO granted-patent dataset, 85.15% of patent data was matched to the KISVALUE firm-level dataset, covering 222,153 patents and 487,876 accumulated citations. Due to incongruence between the patent data and data on company characteristics for KOSDAQ and unlisted companies, this study uses only data on KOSPI-listed firms. Since the matching process effectively linked patents and citations to the KOSPI-listed firms (90.35% of patents and 88.55% of accumulated citations), the authors conclude that limiting the analysis to KOSPI-listed firms does not materially affect the empirical implications of the study.

Of the financialization indicators, RTP is calculated as the ratio of total payout (sum of dividends and stock repurchases) to net profit. RDP is the ratio of dividend payouts to net profit. RFA is defined as the ratio of financial asset investment to tangible assets, with financial asset investment encompassing investment in short- and long-term financial instruments and acquisition of short- and long-term securities trading positions. Finally, RPFA is calculated as the ratio of profit from financial assets to tangible assets. Profit from financial assets is the sum of valuation gains on short-term financial instruments, valuation gains on short-term securities trading positions, valuation gains on securities sales, and valuation gains on other securities. Two of the indicators (RFA and RPFA) were standardized by being divided by tangible assets.

Innovation performance trends

In terms of innovation performance, there were 36,424 applications and 21,684 registrations of Korean patents with WIPO in 2019. Korea ranked third in the world—just after the United States and Japan—on both patent applications and registrations. Furthermore, the number of

Korean patent applications to the USPTO in 2019 was 19,074, ranking Korea in 5th position after China, the United States, Japan, and Germany. Also, Korean inventors submitted 8,332 patent applications and registered 7,251 patents with the EPO (European Patent Office) in 2019, the 6th highest for both applications and registrations.

Table 3.13 summarizes the number of Korean patents by five-year period in individual industries from 2000 to 2019. This industry

Table 3.13 Number of patents by five-year period and industries

	2000–2004	2005–2009	2010–2014	2015–2019
Agriculture, forestry, and fishing	0	0	1	3
Mining and quarrying	0	0	0	0
Manufacturing	14,581	31,860	62,920	98,633
(chemicals and chemical products; except pharmaceuticals and medicinal chemicals)	166	405	1,625	3,713
(electronic components, computer; visual, sounding and communication equipment)	11,872	27,074	51,657	72,896
(electrical equipment)	466	1,500	2,275	3,053
(motor vehicles, trailers, and semitrailers)	559	791	2,058	7,191
Electricity, gas, steam, and air conditioning supply	46	45	604	135
Water supply; sewage, waste management, materials recovery	0	0	0	0
Construction	23	9	25	12
Wholesale and retail trade	144	98	36	301
Transportation and storage	0	5	1	24
Accommodation and food service activities	0	0	0	0
Information and communication	279	208	1,038	3,578
Financial and insurance activities	0	0	1	0
Real-estate activities	20	2	3	0
Professional, scientific, and technical activities	119	263	420	650
others	0	6	66	80
Total	15,212	32,496	65,169	103,416

Source: USPTO database, KISVALUE database

classification is based on KSIC (Korea Standard of Industry Classification). In all five-year periods, the largest numbers of patents were registered by companies in the manufacturing sector (C), followed by the information and communication sector (J). In the manufacturing sector, there were significant increases in chemicals and chemical products (from 166 in 2000–2004 to 3,713 in 2015–2019) and electronic components, computer, visual sounding and communication equipment (11,872 in 2000–2004 to 72,896 in 2015–2019). And electrical equipment increased from 466 in 2000–2004 to 3,053 in 2015–2019.

However, the number of patents registered in a wider range of sectors, such as membership organizations, repair, and other personal services (S), and transportation and storage (H), rose over time. While the number of registered patents went up in most industries, the real-estate activities (L) sector showed a declining trend. During the 2000–2004 period, 20 Korean patents were registered in real-estate activities (L), but this dropped to two patents in 2005–2009 and zero patents in 2015–2019.

Figure 3.2 shows the annual trends for the number of patents registered and the annual sum of their citations. There is a continuous rise in the number of patents registered over the period. For example, the 1,971 patents registered in 2000 rose to 3,557 (2005), 10,323 (2010), 16,491 (2015), and 19,253 (2019). However, the number of accumulated citations followed a different trend. Citations increased from 12,404 in 2000 to 18,798 in 2004. The level then remained stable between 2005 (15,776) and 2012 (14,693), before dropping steeply thereafter. Because accumulated citations are recorded based on the year of patent registration, recently registered patents are likely to have fewer citations than those granted earlier.

The declining number of accumulated citations could result from (1) fewer patents being registered or (2) fewer citations accumulated per patent. Figure 3.3 confirms that the decline is due to the second reason, since the number of accumulated citations per patent fell dramatically over the study period.

Korean patent registrations and accumulated citations resulted from investment in R&D. As of 2019, total R&D investment in Korea was about 76.4 billion USD, 5th in the world after the United States, China, Japan, and Germany. The ratio of R&D to GDP is another indicator of R&D investment, which in 2019 was 4.64%, 2nd in the world after Israel (NTIS).

Figure 3.4 shows the R&D stock of KOSPI-listed firms over time. In this study, R&D stock is calculated using the perpetual inventory method, with a depreciation rate of 0.15, as suggested by Hall et al.

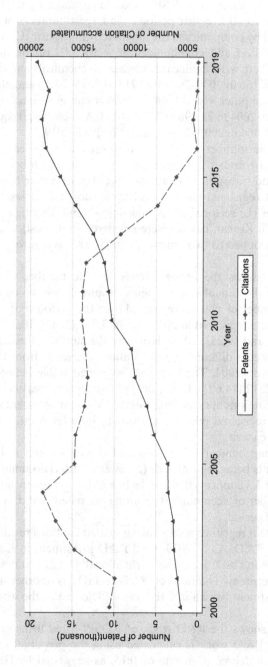

Figure 3.2 Trend of patents registered and their annual citations.
Source: USPTO database.

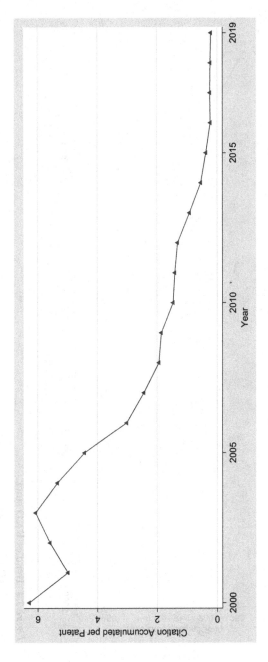

Figure 3.3 Trend of citations accumulated per patent.
Source: USPTO database.

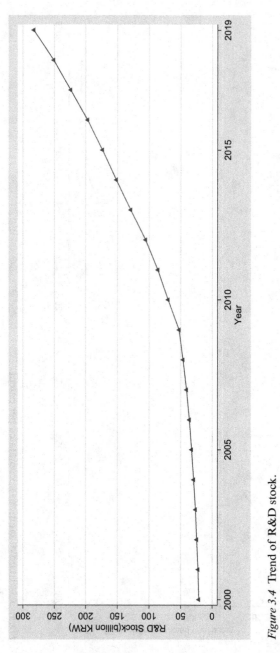

Figure 3.4 Trend of **R&D** stock.

Source: KISVALUE Database.

(2005). R&D stock increased from 21.0 billion KRW (2000) to 70.0 billion KRW (2010) and 202.9 billion KRW (2019). Therefore, it can be inferred that Korea's high patent application and registration rankings were supported by enormous R&D investment by the private and public sectors.

Financialization trends

As introduced above, this study looks at four indicators of financialization.

The first two indicators are based on the composition of total payouts (dividends and stock repurchases). Figure 3.5 shows aggregate dividends and stock repurchases by KOSPI-listed firms. Dividends broadly rose over the study period, even though they dropped off in 2018 and 2019. However, stock repurchase levels were uneven, decreasing until 2014, rebounding in 2015 and 2016, and then dropping again afterward.

Using the first indicator of financialization, Figure 3.6 shows the mean and median trends for the ratio of total payout to net profit (RTP) of KOSPI-listed firms. The mean and median values are shown together to minimize confusion resulting from data fluctuation. RTP is positively correlated with the shareholder value maximization approach and mean values of RTP were generally higher before 2009 than from 2009 onward. Since 2009, mean values have been stable at around 16–17% (Seo, Kang, and Baek, 2020). Median RTP values rose until 2007 and then remained largely stable thereafter at around 12%.

Figure 3.7 shows the mean and median trends for KOSPI-listed firms of the second indicator, the ratio of dividend payouts (RDP). Mean values have fluctuated more than median values, with median values remaining relatively stable at around 6–7%. In addition, the rapid decrease of mean ratio in 2008 was mainly attributed to the global financial crisis that deteriorated the net profit of the KOSPI listed companies.

Figure 3.8 shows the trendline for the financial-asset-investment (RFA) ratio mean of KOSPI-listed firms. Overall, the mean rose through 2014, before dropping. Specifically, values soared from 0.78 (2000) to 3.08 (2005), 5.39 (2010), and 29.63 (2014). They then fell to 20.77 (2015) and again declined to 12.59 (2019). A higher RFA ratio may imply that a company has decreased investment in non-financial assets and technological innovation, which might in turn lead to a deterioration in technological innovation performance.

Finally, the mean ratio of profits of financial assets (RPFA) of KOSPI-listed firms over time is shown in Figure 3.9. The values tended to increase over the years, except for significant drops in 2013 (−0.61)

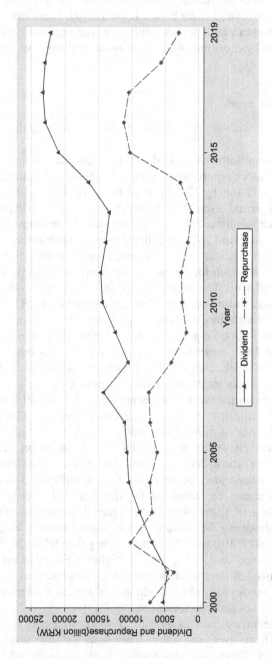

Figure 3.5 Trends of aggregate dividends and repurchases.
Source: KISVALUE database.

P of the plate when the plate is undeformed. Then, the displacement of P after deformation can be expressed in terms of measure numbers u_1, u_2, u_3, as

$$\mathbf{u} = u_1(x_1, x_2, t)\mathbf{r}_1 + u_2(x_1, x_2, t)\mathbf{r}_2 + u_3(x_1, x_2, t)\mathbf{r}_3 \qquad (4.2)$$

Now consider the line elements in Figure 4.1, AP', BP', which are parallel to x_1, x_2, respectively, when the plate is undeformed, with A, B being two points fixed on the edge of the plate (Figure 4.1).

If we restrict our analysis to a plate whose middle surface is inextensible, then the length of these line elements remains constant during deformation of the plate, when the coordinates of P become (ξ_1, ξ_2, t), that is

$$x_1 = \int_0^{\xi_1} \left\{ 1 + \left[\frac{\partial u_2(\sigma, x_2, t)}{\partial \sigma} \right]^2 + \left[\frac{\partial u_3(\sigma, x_2, t)}{\partial \sigma} \right]^2 \right\}^{1/2} d\sigma \qquad (4.3)$$

$$x_2 = \int_0^{\xi_2} \left\{ 1 + \left[\frac{\partial u_1(x_1, \sigma, t)}{\partial \sigma} \right]^2 + \left[\frac{\partial u_3(x_1, \sigma, t)}{\partial \sigma} \right]^2 \right\}^{1/2} d\sigma \qquad (4.4)$$

To save labor in writing, we introduce the symbols J_1 and J_2 as

$$J_1(\sigma, x_2, t) = 1 + \left[\frac{\partial u_2(\sigma, x_2, t)}{\partial \sigma} \right]^2 + \left[\frac{\partial u_3(\sigma, x_2, t)}{\partial \sigma} \right]^2 \qquad (4.5)$$

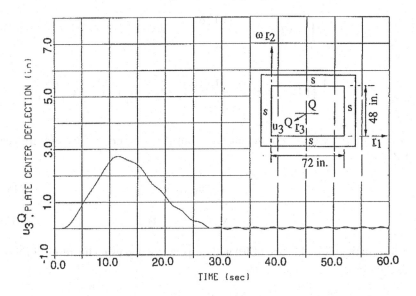

FIGURE 4.2 Transient deflection in inches of the center point u_3^Q of a simply supported plate (supports indicated in the inset by s) spun-up from rest about an edge along $\mathbf{r}_2$ to a maximum spin rate of 12 rpm.

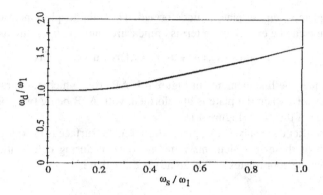

FIGURE 4.3 Ratio of dynamic frequency due to centrifugal stiffening, to first natural frequency, ω_d/ω_1, versus ratio of spin frequency to first natural frequency, ω_s/ω_1, of the plate.

$$J_2(x_1,\sigma,t) = 1 + \left[\frac{\partial u_1(x_1,\sigma,t)}{\partial \sigma}\right]^2 + \left[\frac{\partial u_3(x_1,\sigma,t)}{\partial \sigma}\right]^2 \qquad (4.6)$$

Differentiating under the integral sign in Eqs. (4.3) and (4.4) with respect to t, we get

$$0 = \frac{1}{2}\int_0^{\xi_1}\left[J_1(\sigma,x_2,t)\right]^{-1/2}\frac{\partial J_1(\sigma,x_2,t)}{\partial t}d\sigma + \dot{\xi}_1\left[J_1(\xi_1,x_2,t)\right]^{1/2} \qquad (4.7)$$

$$0 = \frac{1}{2}\int_0^{\xi_2}\left[J_2(x_1,\sigma,t)\right]^{-1/2}\frac{\partial J_2(x_1,\sigma,t)}{\partial t}d\sigma + \dot{\xi}_2\left[J_2(x_1,\xi_2,t)\right]^{1/2} \qquad (4.8)$$

The *instantaneous coordinates* of the point P are related to the coordinates of P′ by

$$\xi_1 = x_1 + u_1(x_1,x_2,t) \qquad (4.9)$$

$$\xi_2 = x_2 + u_2(x_1,x_2,t) \qquad (4.10)$$

Differentiating Eqs. (4.9) and (4.10) with respect to t, and using the results in Eqs. (4.7) and (4.8):

$$\dot{u}_1 = -\frac{1}{2}[J_1(\xi_1,x_2,t)]^{-1/2}\int_0^{\xi_1}[J_1(\sigma,x_2,t)]^{-1/2}\frac{\partial J_1(\sigma,x_2,t)}{\partial t}d\sigma \qquad (4.11)$$

$$\dot{u}_2 = -\frac{1}{2}\left[J_2(x_1,\xi_2,t)\right]^{-1/2}\int_0^{\xi_2}\left[J_2(x_1,\sigma,t)\right]^{-1/2}\frac{\partial J_2(x_1,\sigma,t)}{\partial t}d\sigma \qquad (4.12)$$

Considering points on the line element BP′, we express u_2 and u_3 in series expansions:

$$u_2(\sigma,x_2,t) = \sum_{j=1}^{n}\phi_{2j}(\sigma,x_2)q_j(t) \qquad (4.13)$$

$$u_3(\sigma,x_2,t) = \sum_{j=1}^{n}\phi_{3j}(\sigma,x_2)q_j(t) \qquad (4.14)$$

Similarly, for the line element AP′, we express u_1 and u_3 as

$$u_1(x_1,\sigma,t) = \sum_{j=1}^{n}\phi_{1j}(x_1,\sigma)q_j(t) \qquad (4.15)$$

$$u_3(x_1,\sigma,t) = \sum_{j=1}^{n}\phi_{3j}(x_1,\sigma)q_j(t) \qquad (4.16)$$

The spatial functions $\phi_{1j},\phi_{2j},\phi_{3j}$ $j=1,\dots,n$ introduced in Eqs. (4.13)–(4.16) are as yet unrestricted; ultimately, we will take them to be the vibration mode shapes for a plate with appropriate boundary conditions. The temporal functions $q_j(t)$ ($j=1,\dots,n$) play the role of generalized coordinates in the sense of Lagrange, and n is simply any integer indicating how many functions or modes are kept in the series. Differentiating Eqs. (4.5) and (4.6) with respect to t, and using Eqs. (4.13)–(4.16), we get the following expressions:

$$\frac{\partial J_1(\sigma,x_2,t)}{\partial t} = 2\sum_{i=1}^{n}\sum_{j=1}^{n}[\phi'_{2i}(\sigma,x_2)\phi'_{2j}(\sigma,x_2)$$
$$+\phi'_{3i}(\sigma,x_2)\phi'_{3j}(\sigma,x_2)]\dot{q}_i(t)q_j(t) \qquad (4.17)$$

$$\frac{\partial J_2(x_1,\sigma,t)}{\partial t} = 2\sum_{i=1}^{n}\sum_{j=1}^{n}[\phi'_{1i}(x_1,\sigma)\phi'_{1j}(x_1,\sigma)$$
$$+\phi'_{3i}(x_1,\sigma)\phi'_{3j}(x_1,\sigma)]\dot{q}_i(t)q_j(t) \qquad (4.18)$$

where primes denote the partial differentiation with respect to the dummy space variable σ. Now, substituting Eqs. (4.17) and (4.18) into Eqs. (4.11) and (4.12) gives

$$\dot{u}_1 = -\left[J_1(\xi_1,x_2,t)\right]^{-(1/2)} \int_0^{\xi_1} \left\{ \begin{matrix} [J_1(\sigma,x_2,t)]^{-(1/2)} \times \\ \sum_{i=1}^n \sum_{j=1}^n \begin{bmatrix} \phi'_{2i}(\sigma,x_2)\phi'_{2j}(\sigma,x_2) \\ +\phi'_{3i}(\sigma,x_2)\phi'_{3j}(\sigma,x_2) \end{bmatrix} \dot{q}_i q_j \end{matrix} \right\} d\sigma \qquad (4.19)$$

$$\dot{u}_2 = -\left[J_2(x_1,\xi_2,t)\right]^{-(1/2)} \int_0^{\xi_2} \left\{ \begin{matrix} [J_2(x_1,\sigma,t)]^{-(1/2)} \times \\ \sum_{i=1}^n \sum_{j=1}^n \begin{bmatrix} \phi'_{1i}(x_1,\sigma)\phi'_{1j}(x_1,\sigma) \\ +\phi'_{3i}(x_1,\sigma)\phi'_{3j}(x_1,\sigma) \end{bmatrix} \dot{q}_i q_j \end{matrix} \right\} d\sigma \qquad (4.20)$$

In addition, differentiation of Eq. (4.14) or (4.16) with respect to t yields

$$\dot{u}_3 = \sum_{i=1}^n \phi_{3i}(x_1,x_2)\dot{q}_i \qquad (4.21)$$

The velocity of point P in the Newtonian frame N can now be formally written as

$$^N\mathbf{v}^P = {}^N\mathbf{v}^O + {}^N\boldsymbol{\omega}^R \times \left\{ \begin{matrix} \left[x_1 + \sum_{j=1}^n \phi_{1j}(x_1,x_2)q_j(t) \right]\mathbf{r}_1 \\ + \left[x_2 + \sum_{j=1}^n \phi_{2j}(x_1,x_2)q_j(t) \right]\mathbf{r}_2 \\ + \sum_{j=1}^n \phi_{3j}(x_1,x_2)q_j(t)\mathbf{r}_3 \end{matrix} \right\} \qquad (4.22)$$

$$+ \dot{u}_1\mathbf{r}_1 + \dot{u}_2\mathbf{r}_2 + \dot{u}_3\mathbf{r}_3$$

where $^N\mathbf{v}^O$, $^N\boldsymbol{\omega}^R$, respectively, are the velocity of the point O in N, and the angular velocity of the frame R in N, which can be expressed in terms of the *specified time functions* $v_i(t)$ and $\omega_i(t)$ $(i=1,2,3)$ as follows:

$$^N\mathbf{v}^O = v_1(t)\mathbf{r}_1 + v_2(t)\mathbf{r}_2 + v_3(t)\mathbf{r}_3 \qquad (4.23)$$

$$^N\boldsymbol{\omega}^R = \omega_1(t)\mathbf{r}_1 + \omega_2(t)\mathbf{r}_2 + \omega_3(t)\mathbf{r}_3 \qquad (4.24)$$

Using $\dot{q}_1,...,\dot{q}_n$ as generalized speeds, one can now form the i-th non-linear partial velocity of P in N, by inspection of Eqs. (4.19)–(4.22), as

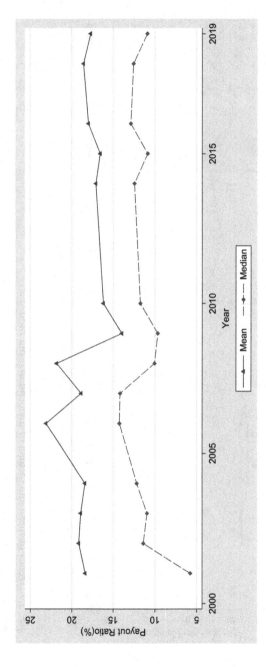

Figure 3.6 Trends of mean and median values of the payout ratio to net profit.
Source: KISVALUE database.

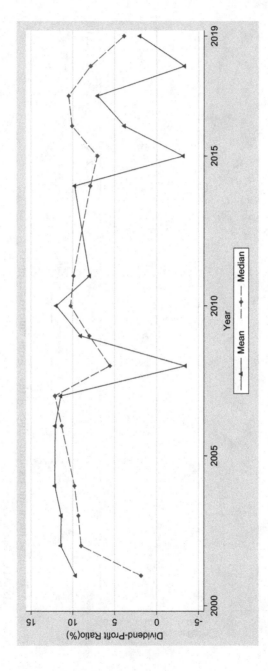

Figure 3.7 Trends of mean and median of dividend to profit ratio.
Source: KISVALUE database.

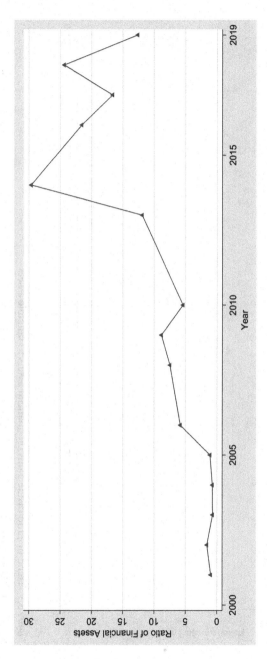

Figure 3.8 Ratio of financial assets to tangible assets.
Source: KISVALUE database.

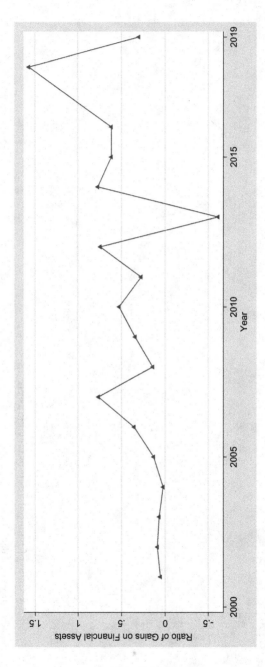

Figure 3.9 Trend of ratio of the gains on financial assets to tangible assets.

Source: **KISVALUE** database.

and 2019 (−0.30). A decrease in 2013 could be explained by volatile foreign situations such as the taper tantrum of the United States and Abenomics of Japan. An increase in the RPFA could indicate an alleviation of financial constraints on a company and this might have a positive impact on investment in innovation, thus fostering firm productivity and greater technological innovation.

References

Hall, B. H., J. Adam, and M. Trajtenberg (2005). "Market value and patent citations," The RAND Journal of Economics, Vol. 36, No. 1, pp.16–38. www.jstor.org/stable/1593752.

IMD World Competitiveness Center. (2021). *Methodology and principles of analysis,* Accessed October 5, 2021. https://worldcompetitiveness.imd.org/rankings/wcy.

Seo, H. J., S. J. Kang, and Y. J. Baek (2020), "Managerial myopia and short-termism of innovation strategy: Financialization of Korean firms," *Cambridge Journal of Economics*, Vol. 44, No. 6, pp. 1197–1220.

Database

IMD World Competitiveness Ranking (www.imd.org/centers/world-competitiveness-center/rankings/world-competitiveness/, retrieved on October 20, 2021).

KISVALUE (www.kisvalue.com/web/index.jsp, retrieved on October 5, 2021).

NTIS (www.ntis.go.kr/rndsts/Main.do, retrieved on October 20, 2021).

OECD database (https://data.oecd.org/, retrieved on October 10, 2021).

USPTO (www.uspto.gov/learning-and-resources/statistics, retrieved on October 15, 2021).

WIPO (www.wipo.int, retrieved on October 15, 2021).

4 Financialization and short-terminism of innovation strategy

Empirical model specification

This study uses negative binomial regression, an analytical approach usually applied to over-dispersed count data with conditional variance higher than the conditional mean. This method is a generalization of Poisson regression, which is restricted by the assumption that the mean and variance are equal.

Equation (4.1) estimates the determinants of firm innovation strategy using negative binomial regression.

$$E[I_{it}|FIN_{it}, X_{it}, \mu_i, \tau_t] = \exp\left(\alpha FIN_{it} + X'_{it}\,\beta + \mu_i + \tau_t\right) \tag{4.1}$$

where I_{it} denotes the level of innovation by firm i at time t. FIN_{it} is an indicator reflecting degree of financialization. X_{it} is the vector of other control variables, and μ_i and τ_t represent firm and year dummies, respectively.

The innovation variable is defined using two indicators. The first is the number of patents granted to firm i in year t. The second is the future-citation-weighted number of patents, meaning the number of citations received by a patent after it has been granted. Together, these two indicators measure both the quantitative aspects of innovation (the number of patents) and the qualitative aspects of innovation (the number of citations). As Trajtenberg (1990) explains, the citation index overcomes the weakness of trying to measure innovation by simply counting the number of patents without considering the quality of those patents.

The degree of financialization is measured using the four indicators described above: RTP, RDP, RFA, and RPFA.

The following control variables were selected based on the literature on innovation performance of firms: R&D stock, export ratio, number of employees, and debt ratio.

DOI: 10.4324/9781003240822-4

First, R&D stock is assumed to be a direct input that produces innovative activities as output. This hypothesis has been asserted under the endogenous growth model (Romer, 1990) and assumes that technological innovation is endogenous and can be affected by own accumulation and R&D inputs such as human capital investment or R&D expenditure.

Second, defined as the ratio of liabilities to tangible assets, the debt ratio reflects the extent of a firm's financial obligations. The effect of debt on a firm's innovation strategy depends on whether the debt ratio is within the financial capacity of the firm to manage. If the debt ratio rises too high, risky projects involving innovation will be postponed, implying that the debt ratio is negatively correlated with innovation performance. However, debt can also finance innovation, which means that the debt ratio could be positively correlated with innovation performance.

Third, the export ratio reflects whether a firm's strategy is oriented toward foreign or domestic markets. The effect of the export ratio on innovation strategy depends on whether Arrow's hypothesis or Schumpeter's hypothesis dominates. Arrow asserts that companies with a higher degree of international exposure face more competition than companies focused more on the domestic market. Therefore, internationally oriented companies will invest more on innovation to survive in the severe conditions of international competition. In this case, the export ratio will be positively correlated with innovation performance. However, Schumpeter suggests a negative correlation between international exposure and innovation activities. Under this logic, if a company is oriented to the domestic market and enjoys a strong monopolistic position there, it will tend to engage in more innovation to increase its monopoly profits.

Fourth, the number of employees is taken to be a proxy of firm size, and firm size is strongly related to market power. Schumpeter hypothesizes that large companies able to invest more in R&D, human capital, and information tend to invest more in innovation activities, meaning that the number of employees is positively related to innovation indicators. However, Arrow counters that firms with higher monopoly power have less incentive to invest in innovation and predicts a negative correlation between the number of employees and innovation performance.

Data and descriptive statistics

Two panel datasets—KISVALUE firm-characteristic data and USPTO patent data—were merged for this analysis. Since the datasets cannot be matched using shared codes, the English names of the companies were used to link the two. Because of difficulties using English names to link unlisted companies and KOSDAQ companies to the patent data, this study uses only KOSPI-listed firms. As of 2019, there were 948 KOSPI-listed firms, 1,510 KOSDAQ companies, and 27,706 unlisted companies in the KISVALUE database.

Table 4.1 lists the summary statistics for the variables used in this empirical model estimation. There are 16,944 observations containing data on the number of patents. In terms of the number of patents registered by a single Korean company, the mean is 11.44, standard deviation is 211.46 with maximum is 9,238. The natural log was taken for the other variables since they are used in log in the estimation process. The number of patents logged has the mean value of 0.17 and standard deviation of 0.79. The accumulated citation as another dependent variable has the mean values of 14.08 and standard deviation of 354.09. Its logged value has the mean value of 0.12 and standard deviation of 0.65.

The Korean firm-level data for 2000–2019 was taken from the KISVALUE database, which includes information to calculate R&D stock, exports, number of employees, and ratios on payouts, dividends, financial assets, gains to financial assets, and liabilities. The information on patent data from 2000 to 2019 was downloaded from the

Table 4.1 Descriptive statistics

Variable	Observations	Mean	Standard deviation	Min.	Max.
Number of patents	16,944	11.44	211.46	0	9,238
ln(number of patents)	16,944	0.17	0.79	0	9.13
Accumulated citations	16,944	14.08	354.09	0	15,675
ln(accumulated citations)	16,944	0.12	0.65	0	9.66
ln(R&D stock)	16,734	14.12	10.82	0	32.53
ln(payout ratio)	13,445	2.29	1.75	−3.44	11.14
ln(dividend ratio)	13,593	2.13	1.69	−3.44	11.14
ln(financial asset ratio)	14,132	0.45	1.01	−1.05	17.77
ln(gains-on-financial-assets ratio)	14,133	0.09	0.44	−0.31	13.89
ln(exports)	13,194	1.93	1.77	0.00	5.23
ln(employees)	14,006	6.08	1.48	0.69	11.56
ln(liability ratio)	14,134	1.36	1.36	0.04	18.22

USPTO website. Accumulated citations of a patent are linked to the year in which the respective patent was granted. As of 2019, the 227,285 patents registered by Korean companies had received 479,626 accumulated citations. Of granted patents, 207,109 (90.35% of total patents registered by Korean companies) are registered by KOSPI-listed firms, these having accumulated a total of 417,951 citations (88.55% of total accumulated citations of patents registered by Korean companies).

After collecting and cleaning the data, English firm names and KISVALUE company codes were used to merge the two panel datasets. If a company was closed through M&A, the patents of the closed company were credited to the acquiring company. As discussed in detail in Chapter 3, due to the difficulties of matching patent data of the USPTO and firm-level variables, this study uses only the KOSPI-listed companies. Ultimately, 85.15% of the USPTO patent panel data was matched to the KOSPI-listed companies from the KISVALUE firm-level panel data for 2000–2019.

Estimation results

Tables 4.2 to 4.5 summarize the estimation results. Tables 4.2 and 4.3 present results using the full sample set for the number of patents registered and the number of citations accumulated, respectively. Tables 4.4 and 4.5 include the estimation results for the number of patents registered and the number of citations accumulated, respectively, but for only the top 25% of firms. Due to the issue of non-concavity of the fixed-effect estimations, all estimation results shown are for random-effect panel analysis with negative binomial estimation.

In Table 4.2, the number of employees (ln(employees)) and R&D stock (ln(R&D stock)) show positive and significant coefficients at the 0.01 significance level, while the impact of exports and debt ratio on the number of patents is statistically insignificant. The number of employees is taken as a proxy of firm size, and the results of the analysis imply that a large workforce promotes innovative activity. Moreover, as a measure of cumulative knowledge of a firm, R&D stock is a significant factor in firm productivity and technological innovation.

Three of the four financialization indicators do not carry statistically significant coefficients. Only the coefficient for gains on financial assets (ln(gains on financial assets)) is shown to be positive and significant at the 0.05 level. This could imply that companies tend to invest earned gains from financial assets on investment in technological innovation, thus showing a positive effect on patent registrations.

Table 4.3 shows the results of the same analysis on the number of citations accumulated, thus reflecting the qualitative indicator of

Table 4.2 Negative binominal regression: Number of patents (full sample)

Variables	Model 1	Model 2	Model 3	Model 4	Model 5
ln(export)	−0.008	−0.018	−0.017	−0.009	−0.007
	(0.015)	(0.016)	(0.016)	(0.015)	(0.015)
ln(employees)	0.531***	0.556***	0.553***	0.535***	0.541***
	(0.047)	(0.050)	(0.049)	(0.048)	(0.048)
ln(R&D stock)	0.047***	0.048***	0.048***	0.047***	0.047***
	(0.007)	(0.007)	(0.007)	(0.007)	(0.007)
ln(debt ratio)	0.113	0.035	0.045	0.099	0.060
	(0.072)	(0.082)	(0.081)	(0.078)	(0.076)
ln(payout ratio)		−0.027			
		(0.018)			
ln(dividend ratio)			−0.015		
			(0.019)		
ln(financial asset ratio)				0.029	
				(0.064)	
ln(gains on financial assets)					0.350**
					(0.139)
Observations	12,864	12,122	12,259	12,862	12,862
Number of firms	775	775	775	775	775

Note: Standard errors shown in parentheses; *** = p<0.01, ** = p<0.05, * = p<0.1.

innovative activities. Unlike the results in Table 4.2, the export ratio is shown here with a positive coefficient, significant at the 0.01 level. This implies that the degree of globalization contributes to promoting quality in innovative activities. Similar to Table 4.2, the impact of the number of employees on accumulated citations is positive and significant, indicating the importance of firm size to the qualitative aspects of innovation. However, the coefficient for R&D stock—a major input of innovation—is statistically insignificant. Further, the debt ratio does not take a statistically significant coefficient.

In contrast to the results in Table 4.3, the coefficients of the following three financialization indicators are negative and significant in Table 4.4: payout ratio (ln(payout ratio)), dividend ratio (ln(dividend ratio)), and gains on financial assets (ln(gains on financial assets)). In other words, higher payout ratio, dividend ratio, and gains on financial assets negatively affect innovative activities, especially the qualitative aspects. The logic for this can be understood as follows. When the financial markets presume firms to boost short-term earnings and stock prices, managers are pressured to direct company funds to dividend payouts and stock repurchases, thus spending less on radical firm innovation.

Table 4.3 Negative binominal regression: Number of citations accumulated (full sample)

Variables	Model 6	Model 7	Model 8	Model 9	Model 10
ln(exports)	0.120***	0.157***	0.153***	0.120***	0.116***
	(0.025)	(0.028)	(0.028)	(0.025)	(0.025)
ln(employees)	0.382***	0.422***	0.431***	0.384***	0.394***
	(0.046)	(0.048)	(0.048)	(0.046)	(0.046)
ln(R&D stock)	0.006	−0.004	−0.004	0.006	0.006
	(0.007)	(0.007)	(0.007)	(0.007)	(0.007)
ln(debt ratio)	−0.207	−0.198	−0.231	−0.233	−0.121
	(0.153)	(0.154)	(0.156)	(0.158)	(0.148)
ln(payout ratio)		−0.048*			
		(0.025)			
ln(dividend ratio)			−0.066**		
			(0.027)		
ln(financial asset ratio)				0.072	
				(0.115)	
ln(gains on financial assets)					−1.160***
					(0.287)
Observations	9,197	8,726	8,833	9,196	9,195
Number of firms	721	721	721	720	721

Note: Standard errors shown in parentheses; *** = p<0.01, ** = p<0.05, * = p<0.1.

The estimation results in Table 4.2 support the argument that pressure to maximize short-term profit or maintain a shareholder-value orientation in management (both reflected by higher payout and dividend ratios) leads to managerial myopia and thus short-termism of corporate innovation strategies in ROK. These results also confirm that greater financial profit leads to short-termism of innovation as well. We can infer from this that Korean companies tend to invest more in financial assets than in R&D or real assets. Thus, decreasing or abandoning R&D efforts requiring large investments over the long run has contributed to short-termism of corporate innovation.

Tables 4.4 and 4.5 show the estimation results using only the top 25% subset, a total of 196 companies. This classification is based on tangible asset value. As in Table 4.2, the number of patents is not affected by the financialization indicators in Table 4.4. Furthermore, the export ratio does not affect the number of patents even though three other independent variables (number of employees, R&D stock, and debt ratio) do take statistically significant coefficients. While the coefficients for

Table 4.4 Negative binominal regression: Number of patents (top 25%)

Variables	Model 11	Model 12	Model 13	Model 14	Model 15
ln(exports)	−0.006	−0.015	−0.014	−0.005	−0.006
	(0.016)	(0.017)	(0.017)	(0.016)	(0.016)
ln(employees)	0.693***	0.701***	0.692***	0.687***	0.695***
	(0.066)	(0.067)	(0.067)	(0.066)	(0.066)
ln(R&D stock)	0.033***	0.035***	0.035***	0.033***	0.033***
	(0.007)	(0.007)	(0.007)	(0.007)	(0.007)
ln(debt ratio)	−0.283**	−0.342***	−0.321***	−0.267**	−0.311***
	(0.116)	(0.120)	(0.120)	(0.120)	(0.117)
ln(payout ratio)		−0.032			
		(0.019)			
ln(dividend ratio)			−0.012		
			(0.021)		
ln(financial asset ratio)				−0.044	
				(0.082)	
ln(gains on financial assets)					0.337
					(0.219)
Observations	3,137	2,974	3,004	3,137	3,137
Number of firms	196	196	196	196	196

Note: Standard errors shown in parentheses; *** = p<0.01, ** = p<0.05, * = p<0.1.

number of employees (ln(employees)) and R&D stock (ln(R&D stock))
are positive at the 0.01 significance level, the coefficient for the debt ratio
(ln(debt ratio)) is negative and significant. This indicates that the quantitative aspects of innovation by the top 25% of firms are particularly
and heavily affected by the debt ratio.

Table 4.5 reports the estimation results for the number of citations
accumulated by the top 25% of firms. While Table 4.3 for the full sample
estimation includes three financial indicators (payout ratio, dividend
ratio, and gains-on-financial-assets ratio) with statistically significant
coefficients, in Table 4.5 all four financialization indicators (payout
ratio, dividend ratio, financial-asset ratio, and gains-on-financial-assets
ratio) play a significant role in influencing the qualitative aspects of
innovation. The estimation results for the control variables in Tables 4.4
and 4.5 (top 25% of firms) are broadly similar to the results in Tables 4.4
and 4.5 (full sample).

To check the robustness of the estimations, three tables in the
Appendix report estimation results for narrower samples: top 10%, top
5%, and bottom 25% of firms. The estimation results on the top 10% and
5% samples for the financialization indicators are generally consistent

Table 4.5 Negative binominal regression: Number of citations accumulated (top 25%)

Variables	Model 16	Model 17	Model 18	Model 19	Model 20
ln(exports)	0.162***	0.207***	0.204***	0.156***	0.168***
	(0.026)	(0.027)	(0.027)	(0.027)	(0.026)
ln(employee)	0.168***	0.241***	0.247***	0.178***	0.170***
	(0.031)	(0.038)	(0.038)	(0.032)	(0.033)
ln(R&D stock)	−0.006	−0.014*	−0.013*	−0.007	−0.004
	(0.006)	(0.007)	(0.007)	(0.006)	(0.006)
ln(debt ratio)	−0.284	−0.354*	−0.354*	−0.399**	−0.074
	(0.188)	(0.191)	(0.191)	(0.200)	(0.195)
ln(payout_ratio)		−0.082***			
		(0.029)			
ln(dividend ratio)			−0.103***		
			(0.031)		
ln(financial asset ratio)				0.236*	
				(0.127)	
ln(gains on financial assets)					−1.042***
					(0.283)
Observations	3,137	2,974	3,004	3,137	3,137
Number of firms	196	196	196	196	196

Note: Standard errors shown in parentheses; *** = p<0.01, ** = p<0.05, * = p<0.1

with the full and top 25% samples. The only important difference is that the payout ratio plays a significant role in innovative activities of the top 25% sample. However, the estimation results on the bottom 25% are not consistent with those of the top 10% and 5% of firms. Only dividend ratio plays a statistically significant role.

Is short-termism of innovation strategy unique to Korea? Or is it a current global trend?

Analyzing patent data from the National Bureau of Economic Research (NBER) for 31 OECD countries (1990–2006), Seo et al. (2020) find that innovation short-termism brought about by financialization is a common phenomenon, not only in Korea, but also in other OECD countries.

In Figures 4.1 and 4.2, the two indicators—ratio of the contribution of financial and insurance activities to total value added (FVA) and ratio of stock market capitalization to GDP (CAP)—are calculated from OECD data to represent degree of financialization. Figure 4.1 shows trends for the United States and for 30 other OECD nations

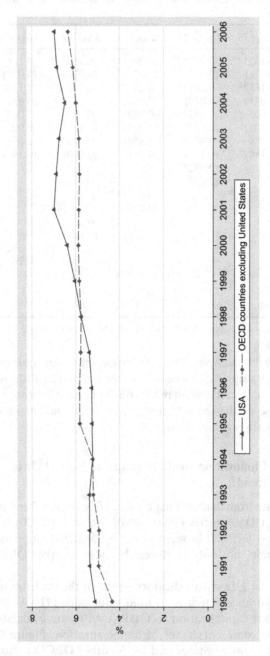

Figure 4.1 Ratio of the contribution of financial and insurance activities to total value added.

Note: Thirty non-US OECD countries: Australia, Austria, Belgium, Canada, Chile, Czech Republic, Denmark, Finland, France, Germany, Greece, Hungary, Iceland, Ireland, Israel, Italy, Japan, South Korea, Luxemburg, Mexico, Netherlands, New Zealand, Norway, Portugal, Spain, Sweden, Switzerland, Turkey, the UK. The country list is the same for all figures (4.2 to 4.6).

Source: NBER Patent DB.

(1990–2006) using FVA, the first variable related to financialization. For both the United States and the other nations, FVA rose continuously. In the United States, this figure rose from 5.1% in 1990 to 7.0% in 2006. In the other OECD countries, it jumped on average from 4.3% to 6.4% over the same period. FVA for the UK (second highest after Luxemburg) edged up from 6.8% in 1990 to 8.3% in 2006. In contrast, FVA in Germany dropped slightly, from 7.0% in 1990 to 4.9% in 2006.

Figure 4.2 presents the trends over the same period for *CAP*, the second financialization variable. *CAP* began at 51.7% (1990) in the United States and reached a peak of 153% in 1999. By 2002, after the IT bubble collapsed, *CAP* had plunged to 100.7%; this was followed by a quick recovery to 141.2% in 2006. For the remaining OECD countries, the second indicator surged from 35.7% in 1990 to 82.9% in 2006, hitting a high of 87.3% in 1999. Results for the UK also followed a similar pattern: 77.7% (1990), 177.4% (1999), and 140.4% (2006). On the other hand, in Germany, where banks have traditionally been the prime source of corporate financing, the second indicator has remained relatively low, from 19.9% in 1990–1994, to 39.98% in 1995–1999, and 54.5% in 2006. Thus, both indicators support the contention that financialization progressed in the United States and other OECD countries during the analysis period.

Discussion about financialization and short-termism of technological innovation strategies also looks at the following aspects. One approach—based on prior research indicating that the number times a patent is cited is positively correlated with its degree of innovation radicalness (Albert et al., 1991)—differentiates between the simple number of patent registrations and the weighted number of patent registrations, the weighting being based on the number of citations for each patent. The *Generality* index proposed by Trajtenberg, Henderson, and Jaffe (1997) is another indicator used to measure the radicalness of innovation, doing so based on the assumption that radicalness is related to the number of different industries and technologies impacted by an innovation since the corresponding patent was registered.

This approach uses five proxy variables for innovation: (1) simple number of patents to reflect the quantitative aspect of patents (*Total*); (2) weighted number of patent registrations based on the number of citations to reflect the qualitative aspects of individual patent (*Cites*); (3) generality; (4) citations per patent (*PCites*); and (5) generality per patent (*PGenerality*). The two variables introduced above (*FVA and*

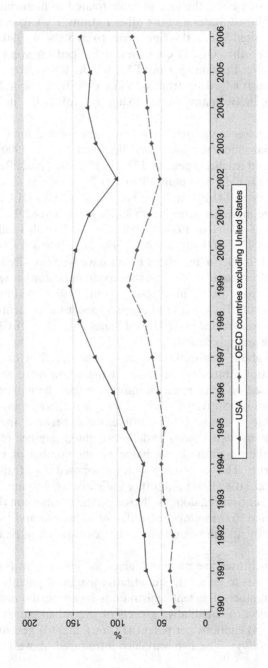

Figure 4.2 Ratio of stock market capitalization to GDP.
Source: NBER Patent DB.

CAP) are also included as indicators of financialization. The analysis estimates and compares the effects of financialization on short-termism of innovation strategy using four different models: GMM estimation, fixed effects, Poisson regression, and negative binominal regression. Figures 4.3–4.6 depict innovation trends for different variables. The trend lines for the total number of patents registered annually in the United States by inventors from all OECD countries between 1990 and 2006 are drawn in Figure 4.3. During the study period, the number of patents registered with the US Patent and Trademark Office by Americans increased by 1.89 times, from 47,391 to 89,823. Patents by applicants from other OECD countries also increased 1.8 times during the same period. The US trend line jumps notably between 1997 and 1998, as the number of patents registered in 1998 (80,289 registrations) was 30% higher than 1997.

Figure 4.4 shows the average forward citations per patent, doing so separately for patents by US inventors and by inventors from other OECD countries. In the United States between 1990 and 1994, there were an average of 11.26 patent citations per patent (*PCites*). But this number later dropped to 9.97 (1995–1999) and 3.71 (2000–2004). For the other OECD countries (i.e. OECD countries, excluding the United States), *PCites* trended downward from 10.09 to 8.27 and 3.13, respectively, over the same period. *PGenerality* for the United States also fell, from 0.41 to 0.39 and 0.24, respectively, also over the same period. Likewise, for Japan, these values declined from 0.47 to 0.43 and 0.25. *PGenerality* for the United States also fell, from 0.41 to 0.39 and 0.24, respectively, also over the same period. Finally, for all non-US OECD countries, the values trended lower, from 0.33 to 0.31 and 0.16.

These findings can be summarized as follows. First, based on measuring the degree of financialization as the ratio of contribution of financial and insurance activities to total value added or as the ratio of stock market capitalization to GDP, financialization progressed rapidly during the analysis period in the OECD countries. Second, the radicalness of technological innovation declined as financialization deepened. This shows that financialization reduces the radicalness of technological innovation, implying that the nature and strategy of technology innovation by corporations has shifted toward a focus on incremental innovation. Third, using the number of patents as the dependent variable produces varying results, which depend on whether this proxy variable reflects quantitative or qualitative aspects of patents. In the former case, the number of patent registrations increases as financialization

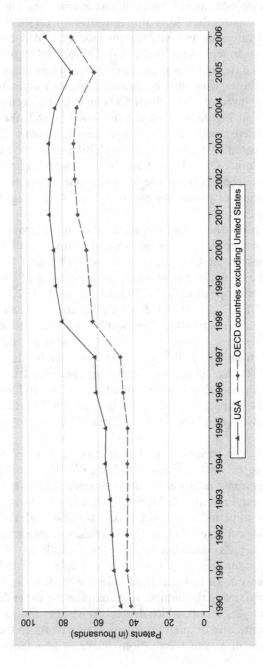

Figure 4.3 Total number of US patent registrations by inventors from non-US OECD countries.
Source: NBER Patent DB.

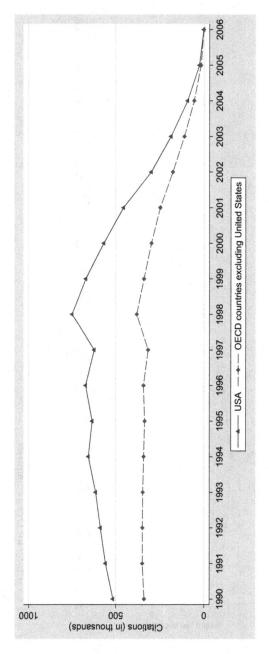

Figure 4.4 Total number of citations of patents registered by inventors from OECD countries.

Source: NBER Patent DB.

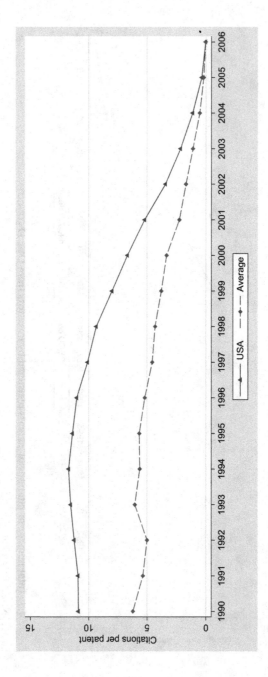

Figure 4.5 PCites for OECD countries.
Source: NBER Patent DB.

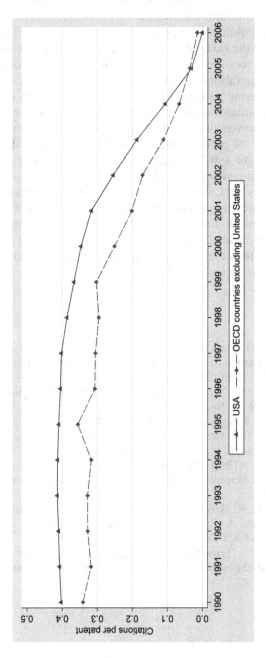

Figure 4.6 P*Generality* values for OECD countries.

88 *Financialization and short-terminism of innovation strategy*

deepens. However, in the latter case, as financialization progresses, the radicalness of innovation decreases.

As patent holdings play a greater signaling role to the financial markets about the value of an enterprise or the success of an IPO, and as the importance of patents as collateral in the financing of enterprises increases, corporations are becoming more aggressive at applying for and registering patents. Thus, the number of patent registrations has increased quantitatively as financialization has taken root in the economy. However, our results show that this quantitative increase in the number of patents reflects a shift toward gradual and minor improvements to existing technologies and away from radical and fundamental innovation. Therefore, even though this study looked at OECD country data, it still reaches conclusions that match the results of our study, which used corporate data. As conditions of managerial myopia worsen in line with deepening financialization, economic entities direct technological innovation strategy toward incremental innovation at the expense of radical innovation, which involves high-risk and long-term investment.

References

Albert, M. B., D. Avery, F. Narin, and P. R. McAllister (1991), "Direct validation of citation counts as indicators of industrially important patents," *Research Policy*, Vol. 20, No. 3, pp. 251–259.

Romer, P.M. (1990), "Endogenous technological change," *Journal of Political Economy*. Vol. 98, No. 5, pp. 71–102.

Seo, H. J., S. J. Kang, and Y. J. Baek (2020), "Managerial myopia and short-termism of innovation strategy: Financialization of Korean firms," *Cambridge Journal of Economics*, Vol. 44, No. 6, pp. 1197–1220.

Trajtenberg, M. (1990), "A penny for your quotes: Patent citations and the value of innovations," *Rand Journal of Economics,* Vol. 21, No. 1, pp. 172–187.

Trajtenberg, M., R. Henderson, and Jaffe, A. (1997), "University versus corporate patents: A window on the basicness of invention," *Economics of Innovation and New Technology*, Vol. 5, No. 1, pp. 19–50.

Tridico, P. (2012), "Financial crisis and global imbalances: Its labor market origins and the aftermath," *Cambridge Journal of Economics*, Vol. 36, No. 1, pp. 17–42.

Database

KISVALUE (www.kisvalue.com/web/index.jsp, retrieved on October 5, 2021).

NBER (www.nber.org/research/data/us-patents, retrieved on October 20, 2021).

OECD database (https://data.oecd.org/, retrieved on October 10, 2021).

USPTO (www.uspto.gov/learning-and-resources/statistics, retrieved on October 15, 2021).

Chapter appendices

Appendix Table 4.1 Negative binominal regression: Number of citations accumulated (top 10%)

Variables	Model 21	Model 22	Model 23	Model 24	Model 25
ln(exports)	0.172***	0.222***	0.219***	0.164***	0.182***
	(−0.03)	(−0.031)	(0.031)	(0.031)	(−0.028)
ln(employee)	0.083**	0.135***	0.147***	0.101***	0.071*
	(−0.037)	(−0.045)	(0.044)	(0.038)	(−0.041)
ln(R&D stock)	0.015	0.009	0.008	0.012	0.021**
	(−0.01)	(−0.011)	(0.011)	(0.010)	(−0.009)
ln(debt)	−0.113	−0.203	−0.214	−0.319	0.349
	(−0.246)	(−0.247)	(0.246)	(0.275)	(−0.269)
ln(payout ratio)		−0.053			
		(−0.035)			
ln(dividend ratio)			−0.085**		
			(0.037)		
ln(financial asset ratio)				0.318*	
				(0.189)	
ln(gains on financial assets)					−1.353***
					(−0.305)
Observations	1,354	1,272	1,282	1,354	1,354
Number of firms	79	79	79	79	79

Note: Standard errors shown in parentheses; *** = p<0.01, ** = p<0.05, * = p<0.1.

Appendix Table 4.2 Negative binominal regression: Number of citations accumulated (top 5%)

Variables	Model 26	Model 27	Model 28	Model 29	Model 30
ln(exports)	0.203***	0.241***	0.235***	0.197***	0.200***
	(0.033)	(0.034)	(0.034)	(0.033)	(0.032)
ln(employee)	0.057	0.101*	0.118**	0.079*	0.049
	(0.046)	(0.054)	(0.054)	(0.047)	(0.048)
ln(R&D stock)	0.042***	0.030**	0.029*	0.040***	0.044***
	(0.014)	(0.015)	(0.015)	(0.014)	(0.013)
ln(debt)	−0.676**	−0.638**	−0.623**	−0.990***	−0.396
	(0.276)	(0.275)	(0.276)	(0.323)	(0.319)
ln(payout ratio)		−0.043			
		(0.045)			
ln(divident ratio)			−0.090*		
			(0.047)		
ln(financial asset ratio)				0.420*	
				(0.227)	
ln(gains on financial assets)					−0.597*
					(0.336)
Observations	726	679	685	726	726
Number of firms	40	40	40	40	40

Note: Standard errors shown in parentheses; *** = p<0.01, ** = p<0.05, * = p<0.1.

Appendix Table 4.3 Negative binominal regression: Number of citations accumulated (bottom 25%)

Variables	Model 31	Model 32	Model 33	Model 34	Model 35
ln(exports)	−0.035	0.120	0.189***	−0.048	0.001
	(0.306)	(0.395)	(0.022)	(0.306)	(0.307)
ln(employee)	0.837	0.649	0.381***	0.853	0.736
	(0.562)	(0.681)	(0.044)	(0.565)	(0.568)
ln(R&D stock)	0.409*	0.338	−0.012*	0.430*	0.385*
	(0.216)	(0.237)	(0.006)	(0.224)	(0.205)
ln(debt ratio)	−1.727*	−1.509	−0.109	−1.752*	−1.721*
	(1.001)	(1.062)	(0.129)	(0.990)	(0.930)
ln(payout ratio)		0.038			
		(0.190)			
ln(dividend ratio)			−0.100***		
			(0.025)		
ln(financial asset ratio)				0.256	
				(0.688)	

Appendix Table 4.3 Cont.

Variables	Model 31	Model 32	Model 33	Model 34	Model 35
ln(gains on financial assets)					1.700 (1.172)
Observations	3,129	2,911	9,297	3,128	3,128
Number of firms	191	191	584	191	191

Note: Standard errors shown in parentheses; *** = p<0.01, ** = p<0.05, * = p<0.1.

5 Conclusion

We analyzed the interaction between financialization and corporate innovation strategy, exploring this relatively new topic for two reasons. First, we shed new light on the role of financialization on innovation. Previous studies on financialization have looked at the effects of financialization on corporate governance, economic growth, investment in real assets, the labor market, and income inequality. However, the relationship between financialization and technological innovation, and especially corporate innovation strategy, has not been investigated in much depth. Therefore, this book analyzed the channels through which financialization affects the technological innovation strategy of companies. Based on this analytical framework, we looked specifically at how financialization has affected the innovation strategies of Korean companies and considered predictions about the impact financialization will continue to have in the future.

The second reason is related to the current situation of Korean companies and their futures. Leading Korean companies such as Samsung, Hyundai, LG, and SK, which have transformed themselves into global multinationals, have carried out past technological innovation based on a catch-up strategy. This involves accumulating technological capabilities by imitating or reverse engineering products developed in advanced countries. However, as leading Korean companies gradually improve their innovative capabilities and approach the global technology frontier, they are now positioned to shift the technology frontier itself through radical, or fundamental, innovation. In addition to the burden of being technology leaders under the existing paradigm, the so-called *chaebol* companies of Korea are also participating in setting future technology standards, striving to become leaders under new paradigms of AI, IoT, 5G, big data, and other technologies related to the Fourth Industrial Revolution. As detailed in the literature on technological innovation, trying to make radical innovations and competing in setting technology

DOI: 10.4324/9781003240822-5

standards involve many uncertainties and risks. Therefore, our second reason for writing this book is to examine how and under what institutional conditions Korean companies might succeed as they face these challenges full of uncertainty and risk.

How does financialization affect a company's technological innovation strategy?

Even as emerging evidence is showing how financialization impacts areas of the economic domain—corporate governance, corporate investment strategy, income inequality, global economic crises, labor markets— research into the relationship between financialization and technological innovation remains underdeveloped. Notably, the following questions remain: Has financialization transformed the relationship between finance and corporate innovation strategy? If so, through which channels has this transformation been affected? Rather than providing complete answers to these questions, this book focuses on changes in the relationship between financial markets and non-financial companies (NFCs) and on changes in corporate governance, doing so by analyzing the impact of financialization on corporate innovation strategy. We consider the impact of financialization on technological innovation through the linked relationships between "financialization," "managerial myopia," and "short-termism of innovation strategy," focusing on Korean companies. Short-termism of innovation strategy refers to changes in the characteristics of technological innovation strategy resulting from greater firm focus on incremental innovation, compared to radical innovation.

We propose that financialization and managerial myopia can negatively impact corporate innovation strategy through the following three paths.

First, as shareholder value becomes more important, managers prioritize efforts to raise stock prices and earn short-term returns, and these efforts lead to an increase in dividend payouts and stock buybacks. Rather than increasing investment to enhance long-term competitiveness of the company, managers pay more attention to dividends and share buybacks to increase stock prices and short-term returns. However, this shareholder value-priority management approach by managers ensures that a large portion of a company's net profit is allocated to dividends and share buybacks rather than investments. As a result, the company's investment in R&D decreases, and the innovation planning horizons of NFCs shorten.

Under the second path, financial innovation has encouraged development of a variety of new financial commodities, which has increased the opportunity for firms to raise profits by investing in financial assets. Thus, the income earned by companies by investing in financial assets has increased in recent years; in turn, NFCs have come to hold more financial assets that generate high profits in the short term and have cut back on investments in R&D and intangible assets. Furthermore, as companies increase their investments in financial assets, the rate of return required by financial markets continues to rise. As a result, innovation projects unlikely to meet market-dictated required rates of return, likely to take a long time to pay off, or burdened by high risk have been downsized or cancelled.

Lastly, the rise of a shareholder value orientation has pushed corporate innovation strategy toward a short-term perspective, putting less emphasis on the long term. Capital market pressure and shareholder impatience force managers to keep their eyes on short-term performance. As a result, managers adjust corporate strategy to match policies focused on incremental innovation delivering adequate results with lower R&D spending. This approach contrasts with radical innovation, which does not contribute to business results in the short term, is highly risky, and requires large R&D investments over a long period of time before performance gains can be realized.

The first two paths describe how financialization negatively impacts innovation by reducing investment in R&D and intangible assets, as well as in real investments. However, the third mechanism suggests that financialization can also change the nature of corporate innovation strategy itself. In other words, as the emphasis on shareholder value and capital-market pressures have promoted short-termism by companies, firm strategy would be expected to have shifted toward incremental innovation focused on gradual improvements, rather than on radical innovation that is accompanied by high risk and long-term investment outlays.

How has financialization affected the technological innovation strategies of Korean companies?

Our study empirically examines whether managerial myopia leads to short-termism of innovation strategy, doing so using Korean firm-level and USPTO data covering the period 2000–2019. Financialization is measured using two categories of indicators related to payouts and financial investment. The dividend payout ratio and total payout ratio variables are used as proxies for payouts. Financial asset investment and financial profit are used as proxies for financial investment. In addition, the number of patents registered with the USPTO and the number of accumulated citations are used to measure innovation performance. While the former metric represents the quantitative aspect of innovation performance, the latter encompasses the qualitative aspect of innovation that we are most interested in. When innovation performance was measured by the number of patent registrations, three of the financialization variables (dividend payout ratio, total payout ratio, and financial asset investment ratio; but not the financial profit ratio) were not statistically significant. The analysis results for financial profit support the financial constraints hypothesis. Financial profit from financial asset investment provides a new channel for internal funding and thus helps to relax financial constraints for innovation. On the other hand, when innovation performance is measured by the number of accumulated citations, all three variables related to financialization (except for the financial asset investment ratio) are shown to have a negative effect on the radicalness of innovation. This estimation result confirms that managerial myopia and short-termism of innovation strategy are related.

Is increasing short-termism of innovation strategy a current global trend?

We find through empirical analysis that managerial myopia is brought about by financialization through short-termism of innovation strategies of Korean companies. These findings suggest the need to consider whether short-termism of innovation strategy is unique to ROK or whether it is a global phenomenon among countries under the influence of financialization. Based on the results of Lee et al. (2020), we confirmed that short-termism of corporate innovation strategy due to financialization is not only a phenomenon in ROK but is also commonly observed in OECD countries.

First, by measuring financialization with two variables (ratio of contribution of financial and insurance activities to total value and ratio of stock market capitalization to GDP), Lee et al. (2020) find that financialization has progressed rapidly in all OECD countries, including the United States and the EU, since the 1990s. The authors also found that although the number of patents registered with the USPTO by OECD countries continued to rise, variables linked to the radicalness of innovation (number of citations per patent and the patent generality index) have declined sharply since the mid-1990s. This confirms that financialization and radicalness of innovation have moved in opposite directions. In other words, as financialization progresses, innovation in OECD countries is gradually moving toward incremental innovation and away from radical or fundamental innovation.

Similar to our book empirically analyzing short-termism of corporate innovation strategy based on firm data, the study conducted by Lee et al. confirm that financialization has brought about short-termism of innovation even when analyzed using OECD data. Therefore, as financialization progresses, corporate strategy in OECD countries, including ROK, has been confirmed to be gradually moving away from a focus on radical innovation involving high risk and long-term investment to an incremental innovation approach accompanied by low cost, low risk, and short-term results.

What kind of financial system will enable Korean companies to prosper in the creative destruction process?

Contrary to assumptions under the linear model of technological innovation, technological progress is not a simple process influenced only by developments in S&T and the existence of star scientists and engineers alone does not guarantee the success of innovation. Innovation is a complex and interactive process that requires cooperation and coordination among various stakeholders and institutions. Because uncertainties about the potential of technology, consumer demands, and market conditions are inherent in the innovation process, patient investors and financial institutions are essential to the success of innovation. If investors or financial institutions withdraw or reduce their investments in R&D projects believing it will be difficult to earn adequate profits in the short term, some fundamental innovation efforts that take a long time and are accompanied by high uncertainty will not be undertaken. For example, without investors and financial institutions patiently maintaining a long-term investment horizon, platform-based companies such as Amazon, Facebook, Google, and Apple would not have survived the long years during which they searched for profitable business models and executed on those models, and it would have been impossible for them to achieve the huge profits they are earning today.

As with platform building, there are many uncertainties in the development of 5G, IoT, and AI technologies. Notably, standards have not yet been established for these technologies. Therefore, companies doing business in this space face enormous risks while standards are forming. The existence of patient financial institutions willing to sustain investment while enduring such uncertainty and risk is a key factor of success in the new technology paradigm.

Korean companies and the government hope to gain an edge in new technology paradigms, even as they advance the technology frontier in existing paradigms. For this, it is argued that the training of star scientists and engineers should be given priority. This position is based on the traditional linear model of innovation that emphasizes scientific and technological development within the laboratory. However, other research on financialization and managerial myopia, as well as the current study, presents a more complex picture. Many factors contribute to success in creative destruction under both existing and new technology paradigms. Establishment of proper corporate governance structure and other institutional frameworks, as well as the participation of patient investors, act to reduce uncertainty and encourage entrepreneurship, thus allowing companies to execute management and innovation plans from a long-term perspective.

Reference

Lee, Y. S., H. S. Kim, and H. J. Seo (2020), "Financialization and innovation short-termism in OECD countries," *Review of Radical Political Economics*, Vol. 52, No. 2, pp. 259–286.

Database

OECD database (https://data.oecd.org/, retrieved on October 10, 2021).
USPTO (www.uspto.gov/learning-and-resources/statistics, retrieved on October 15, 2021).

Index

Printed in the United States
by Baker & Taylor Publisher Services